How to Find Your Treasure

in a

Gift Basket

A Step-by-Step Guide to Starting
a Profitable Gift Basket Business

by Ron Perkins

Home Income Publishing
2796 Harbor Blvd. Suite 107
Costa Mesa, CA 92626

How to Find Your Treasure
in a
Gift Basket

by Ron Perkins

Published by:

Home Income Publishing
2796 Harbor Blvd. Suite 107
Costa Mesa, CA 92626

ISBN 0-9627185-1-3

About This Book

Most people who start gift basket services are attracted to the fun aspect of the business, i.e. the fact that it's enjoyable to create the baskets and watch people receive them as gifts. But the gift basket makers who operate profitably all have one thing in common: They all understand that it's a business like any other business, and therefore it requires a good deal of planning and hard work in order to be successful.

This book concentrates on the business side of making gift baskets and strives to give the vital ground-floor knowledge that will save time and money when launching a gift basket company. Read through it carefully and consider how each chapter applies to your own business goals.

The information presented here has been compiled from a number of sources: interviews with successful gift basket entrepreneurs, industry suppliers, trade associations, and advice solicited from experts in the fields of advertising and business consulting. It would take an individual hundreds of dollars in phone calls and weeks of research time to assemble all this information, so we're proud we can offer it all to you in such a concise, informative package.

As you will see when reading this book, a gift basket business can be started at home for little or no up-front investment, or it could require thousands of dollars if you choose to open up a retail gift basket store. Regardless of how much money you plan to commit to your new company, it's always a good idea to consult with an accountant or lawyer before investing anything. Best wishes in your new basket business!

Table of Contents

Introduction

Custom Gift Baskets: Profit from Personalization

Finding the "perfect" gift for someone often requires more than just money; it requires a great deal of time and effort to scout boutiques and shopping malls. To take this hassle out of gift giving, a swelling number of custom gift basket services have arisen from the back rooms of gift shops and the kitchen tables of creative part-time businesspeople to become one of today's hottest low-investment service businesses.

According to one gift basket operator, the business has always been profitable, but in the last few years she has seen an explosion of interest from consumers. If fact, the dollar volume of this person's gift basket business doubled every year from 1982 to 1987 before leveling off. Another large franchised gift basket operation reports that its best stores bring in gross annual sales of $300,000 to $400,000.

Often started with a few hundred dollars—the cost of printing business cards and advertising flyers—custom gift basket services offer an ideal part-time business that has the potential to develop into a full-time profit generator. As a business concept, it's the epitome of simplicity: the customer explains the specific items he or she would like to give and the basket customizer finds these items and incorporates them into an attractive-looking basket, complete with cellophane wrapping and large bow. Or the customer gives a general idea of what the recipient likes and lets the gift basket customizer come up with a list of items to include in the basket.

"Someone will call up and tell me that they need a custom basket made for their mother-in-law's birthday, for example, and then give me all the details on what she likes, her favorite colors, etc., and we'll assemble a basket from this information," explains Yavonne Arranaga, whose California-based company makes gift baskets and custom balloon arrangements.

Arranged inside a sturdy wicker basket, these custom gifts can include everything from gourmet candies and fine wines to perfumes, children's toys, custom stationery, and just about any other gift item, depending upon the wishes of the customer and the recipient of the gift. Prices range from under $20 to over hundreds of dollars for gift baskets that include expensive champagne and silver ice buckets.

One gift basket maker, for example, was asked to make a basket for a hospitalized two-year-old boy. After much care and thought, this basket was packed full of all the right items to make it a special gift for the boy: a hand puppet, a toy truck, a blackboard and chalk, coloring books, candy, bubble gum, and crayons. And everywhere possible, the items were marked with the child's name on them. The entire collection of goodies was "shrink wrapped" and tied with a large bow.

Aside from the personal touch offered by a custom basket, many gift basket creators have noted that another strong reason behind the rapid growth of the gift basket industry is that people like to feel they're "getting something for their money" when they buy a gift. Flowers, for example, won't last more than a few days, whereas the items included in a gift basket are for the most part either edible or reusable.

Because such a wide variety of products can go into these baskets, custom gift basket companies often purchase most of the items at the normal retail price and derive their profit margin by charging for the amount of time it takes to assemble a basket. The exception to this would be ready-made fruit and nut gift baskets, which can be assembled in quantity, and thus can use items that are bought at a quantity wholesale price.

A basket for which the customer ultimately pays $80, for example, will usually require an expenditure of $40 to $50 for the purchase of all the various items going into it. And while this price might seem expensive for a basket full of items that usually can be purchased at the corner market, more and more shoppers want the personalized touch a gift basket offers and don't mind paying someone else to put it together. This is especially true for corporate customers.

"These baskets really make excellent business gifts because there're very few other things a businessman can give to a number of people that each of them will like, so it takes a lot of the hassle out of planning business gifts," says the owner of a thriving custom gift basket shop in Southern California.

This woman started her shop 16 years ago when she supplied all the ready-made gift baskets for an upscale supermarket in her neighborhood. Since that time, she has expanded to a retail storefront and added gift wrapping services and a wide selection of gift products. She also began offering her services to the business community, which proved to be very lucrative: "Many of our corporate clients will call up, for example, and say they need X amount of gifts for their customers or clients, so we find out what they want in the basket and assemble a number of them at one time."

As examples of the types of baskets created for these corporate clients, she recalls how her company made little wheelbarrows full of beer and ham for a construction company, and frequently makes baskets of champagne or mineral water and champagne glasses for law firms to give to their clients after a successful case and doctors to give to their patients after surgery.

As with most custom gift basket shops, the price this woman charges for each of these basket creations ranges from $40 to $150, with the price dependent upon the cost of the items included and the labor time necessary to construct the gift. "Some of these corporate baskets can get very expensive," she explains, "but it's worth it to these companies because they use them as sales tools to build a good relationship with their customers."

Although most successful gift basket operations ultimately end up in a retail store space, this is a business that someone can easily start at home. Since most of the items for each custom basket are purchased only when the customer orders a basket, there's no need to maintain much of a product inventory. And, word-of-mouth referrals will provide a surprising amount of new customers, so advertising costs can also be kept to a minimum during the start-up phase.

In the following chapters of this book, you'll learn how to set up your gift basket service for a minimum initial investment, where to buy many of the supplies and wrapping ingredients for low wholesale prices, some great ideas for custom "theme" baskets, and some low-cost ways to market your service to the people most likely to become customers. You'll notice that the Suppliers section and the Advertising section are two of the longest chapters in this manual and require the most thorough reading, since these represent the most important facets of this business to learn before starting out.

Once your gift basket business is up and running, you'll find what many profitable gift basket companies have found: The business can be a year-round money maker, and not just something for the Christmas season. And, it also can be an emotionally rewarding occupation, since gift baskets are such an appreciated present to receive.

Your Typical Day in Business

Working Out of The Home

Because you'll probably start your gift basket service as a home-based business, without the support of part-time employees, you'll need to establish a daily routine that makes the best use of your time. Most people running "one-man" gift basket businesses use their morning hours to deliver finished baskets to customers and shop for the ingredients needed to complete baskets on order. Figure on making a maximum of two to three deliveries per hour. During this time, the answering machine receives any customer calls and explains that all calls will be returned in the afternoon.

The message for the answering machine should go something like this: "Hello, thank you for calling (your business name). We are away from our office right now but will check all messages this afternoon and return your call later today. Please leave your name and telephone number, and the time of call."

Once you return home from the morning deliveries, spend your time in the afternoon returning calls and assembling baskets. Some of this time should also be set aside for marketing efforts, such as designing direct mail pieces and ads, sending out press releases, stuffing direct mail envelopes, and making follow-up telephone calls to potential corporate clients to whom you've already sent promotional brochures.

You'll quickly learn to prioritize your orders, so that the ones with the most urgent delivery schedule or a long list of ingredients will take first priority over the less urgent basket orders. Each day look through the orders that must be delivered the following day to get an idea of which ones to attend to first. To help with this prioritizing, try setting up a bulletin board where you can pin up a separate index card for each order and arrange the cards in the order that they must be delivered. This way, you can make notes on each card in reference to any extra ingredients that still have to be purchased for a particular order, or any special delivery instructions.

Keep accurate records of your actions to avoid confusion. Mark down a list of all the ingredients and supplies you must buy each day for your baskets, and keep a logbook of all the deliveries you plan to make during the day, noting the person's name, address, company name if it's to be delivered to a corporate client, and phone number in case you get lost trying to find the customer's address.

If you're shipping baskets to recipients out of your regular delivery area, you must also schedule time to stop by your local United Parcel Service office and drop off the basket. Once you build up your volume of UPS shipments, you can open an account with them, so that their truck will stop by your business address once every day to pick up shipments. This daily pick-up service costs around $4 per week extra, but is usually well worth this amount, since it will save you from having to drive down yourself to the UPS office to ship out baskets.

If you have a personal computer, use it to assist you in record-keeping. Over the long run, a computer will save a great deal of time when it comes to storing "databases" of customers, gift recipients, suppliers' names and addresses, corporate "leads" to whom you've sent promotional material, and other valuable information that needs to be accessed on a regular basis.

Taking Basket Orders

As a home-based business, most of the basket orders will come via the telephone, as opposed to people coming to your home. Because of this, many of your sales will be a two-step process, where the customer calls in and you send out a flyer that shows photos of some of your standard theme baskets. You then will call the customer back after a few days to get their order. Or you can make an appointment to go to the customer's location and show an album of photos depicting your basket creations.

Obviously, you should try to get the customer to commit to an order when you first talk to him or her during their initial call. To increase your percentage of orders on the first call, have an itemized list available of all the ingredients in each of your standard theme baskets, in addition to a list of some of the gourmet food items you often include in custom baskets. Having such a list handy when on the phone will enable you to do a better job of describing the baskets and thus increase the likelyhood that the customer will order right then instead of waiting to see samples first.

Also make up a standard order form and xerox some copies to use while on the phone with a customer. This form should have the date, customer's name, mailing address, telephone number, type of basket he wants, estimated price, and the address where the basket will be delivered. Take the time to fill in all of this information with each customer, since it will become valuable to your advertising mailing list. A sample of this type of order form is shown at the end of this chapter.

When a customer wants you to create a custom basket, you'll need to get some specific information before you can proceed. Ask the customer for what occassion the basket is being given as a gift; the age and sex of the recipient; the recipient's hobbies, favorite color, occupation, etc. Find out as much as possible about the recipient, so you can really customize the basket for him or her. Also, find out what type of products they would like to see included in the basket. Should you include personal care products, gourmet foods, wine or other alcoholic beverages, chocolates, etc.? And, finally, find out the price range the customer is willing to spend for the gift.

When dealing with a customer, remember that they are looking to you as a creative consultant to their gift needs, someone who can ingest all the specific facts they give you about the gift recipient and come up with a gift basket perfectly tailored to their needs.

The last step is to inquire into the customer's budget for the basket, since the price estimate will vary considerably depending upon the ingredients used in the basket. Get a feel of how flexible the customer is when it comes to this price estimate. Is he or she more concerned with providing a luxurious gift, or one that strictly adheres to the budget framework specified?

Specify the time you'll need to complete the customer's basket. If you're not busy, you should be able to handle most orders in two to three days. During the busy Thanksgiving and Christmas season, however, you might need up to a week to complete an order. Make sure your customer knows this beforehand and doesn't expect the basket the next day. After a short while, you'll learn to feel out the situation when consulting with customers and make them feel good about their baskets and the price they pay for them.

Ask your customers to pay you upon receipt of their finished basket, whether you deliver it to them or they come to your home or store to pick it up. Be wary of extending credit to new customers, since a few bad accounts could seriously affect your business profitability during the start-up months, and it can be difficult to collect on these accounts.

If a new customer orders by phone and wants the basket shipped to someone outside of your normal delivery area, ask the customer to send you a check up front for the order before shipping the basket. This way, you'll make sure to have the check in your hand before spending any time and money on the basket. If the customer objects to this, tell them to come to you personally and drop off a check when the basket is done, and then you'll drop it off at the U.P.S. office for shipment. Remember to add the freight charges onto the total price of your basket when it is to be shipped to the recipient, in addition to the cost of the box and the filler used for packing the box.

Accepting Credit Cards

Marketing studies have shown that a business that accepts credit card payments makes it more convenient for customers to pay and thus closes more sales. It's a win/win situation for both the business owner and the customer: you're offering credit to your customer, but don't have to personally hassle with collections or billing, since that will be handled by the credit card company.

In theory, the procedure for accepting VISA and MasterCard payments is fairly simple: You get an "imprinter" machine with your business's name and "merchant number" on it. When a customer pays with a credit card, you put the card in the imprinter along with a blank credit card slip and imprint the store information onto the slip. At this point, you also call in the credit card number to a special toll-free phone number, read the credit card number to an operator, who then checks to make sure it's not stolen or charged over its limit. The operator gives you an authorization number, which you write on the credit card sales slip. At the end of the day, you take these slips into the bank that issued you the merchant number and they'll credit your account for the amount of the transactions, less a few percentage points as a service charge.

Unfortunately, most banks have tightened up their requirements for issuing new merchant accounts to businesses that want to begin accepting VISA and Master-Card. Most banks need to see the personal financial statement of the business owner and prefer to issue cards to a company that's already been in business for a while. Check with the bank where you have your gift basket business savings and checking accounts to find out about their prerequisites. Also, check with the Gift and Decorative Accessories Association to see if they offer any assistance to new association members who would like to accept credit cards at their business. Their phone number and address are listed in the Appendix section of this manual.

American Express merchant accounts are a little bit easier to set up than VISA and MasterCard accounts, but require a different procedure for collecting payment. After each day, or week, you total up the American Express receipts for that time period and send them to the credit card company. They will issue you one weekly or monthly payment, depending upon what you specify and will deduct a service charge of one to six percent, depending upon the volume of business you do with American Express cards.

Pricing

It's always difficult for the first-time business owner to figure out the correct price to charge customers for a service: Obviously, you don't want to price your baskets too high, or you'll drive customers away. And you certainly won't stay in business too long if your price your services too low.

To compute a reasonable price for each of your baskets, always keep in mind the following factors:

- cost of materials
- overhead expenses of business
- delivery or shipping charges
- expected profit margin

First, let's look at the cost of the materials that go into the basket. If you have included items you bought at the normal retail price, you really can't mark these up in price. If this is the case, then your profit for the job will come from marking up your price to cover the labor time it takes to shop for the ingredients and assemble the basket. Although the customer only knows the one overall price you quote him, you must separate the material and labor costs of each job in your mind in order to keep track of the net profit accurately.

If you buy basket ingredients in volume at a wholesale cost , such as a brand of wine or preserves, you can make a larger profit margin on each job because you are able to mark up the cost of the goods from your wholesale price to a higher retail price. So, if you were figuring the price on a particular basket where you bought all the ingredients for a wholesale cost of $15.00, but the retail price on these goods is $22.00, then use the $22.00 figure when computing your cost of materials. Thus, you've added an extra $7.00 to your profit, but not charged the customer any more for these items than he or she would have to pay if they went to the store themselves and bought them.

When figuring how to value your labor time in constructing the baskets, you will be influenced most significantly by the prices your competition is charging and your intuition on what the market will bear. The one thing you must do in working out the value of your labor, and thus the amount of mark-up on a particular basket, is to consider your general business "overhead," i.e. the cost of phone bills, advertising, rent, and any other business expense that can't be directly tied to a particular basket in the same way as the cost of ingredients can be.

To estimate overhead expenses, look at how many baskets you sell, or plan to sell, in a particular month and the total cost of the ingredients that go into these baskets, then see what percentage of this figure corresponds with your overhead expenses for a month. For example, if you spend $2,000 for the ingredients to go into your baskets during an average month, and you also spend an average total of $400 per month on advertising, phone bills, and all the other general business expenses, then the overhead percentage is 20% of your cost of materials ($400 is 20% of $2,000).

Once you've got a relative idea of the overhead costs you can apply it to your pricing strategy. To illustrate how this works, you figure the material cost of a particular custom gift basket will be $30. To this figure you then must add your averaged overhead mark-up, which is in this case 20% of the material cost. So now you add $6.00 to your material cost, since 20% of $30 equals $6.00. What this now means is that just to break even on this particular job, you'll have to charge $36.00.

Of course you want to do more than break even; you want to make a profit! After totalling the material cost and the overhead mark-up, add on the profit margin, which could range anywhere from 20% to 100%, depending upon what the market will bear. Generally, smaller baskets that retail for $20 to $40 can be sold at a profit margin of up toward 100%, whereas larger, more expensive baskets will usually provide a smaller profit percentage, in the range of 30% to 50%.

Another factor to consider when figuring on your price is the fact that you shouldn't be afraid to offer some high-end ready made gift baskets in the $125 to $150 range. Although most ready made, or non-customized, gift baskets are priced from $30 to $75, many customers will go for a higher priced gift if it's available and looks like it warrants the extra expense. It also helps the image of your gift basket company to have some of these upscale baskets in your repertoire of available gifts.

Planning for Major Holidays

One fact about the gift basket business is that there are definite "peak" seasons throughout the year where business surges beyond the normal level. Valentine's

Day, of course, represents one such time, as does Christmas. In order to make the most of these seasons and handle a large amount of customers a gift basket maker needs to plan well in advance to make the business run as smoothly as possible. This becomes especially important for Valentine's Day, where almost all of the basket orders will have to be delivered on that one day!

To plan ahead for such a busy time, you'll need to think about three primary concerns: creating ready-made theme baskets, ordering supplies in advance, and your delivery system.

In planning for Valentine's Day, for example, the first step is to think up four or five standard theme baskets that you can sell to customers. By standardizing your theme baskets, you will know ahead of time what ingredients to order in bulk well before February 14th rolls around. This occasion usually requires one or more versions of both romantic and humorous baskets that men can give to women and, likewise, humorous and romantic gift baskets that a woman can give to a man. Popular gift items for these baskets include: champagne, chocolate, roses, perfume, cologne for men, bath soaps and fragrances, lingerie and sexy underwear, and hear-shaped cookies.

Once you've come up with a selection of standard them baskets, the next step is to line up your supply sources for the various gift items and wrapping materials needed to create each of these baskets in quantity. You should do this early (up to a month or two in advance) because many suppliers get swamped with orders before certain holidays and need as much time as possible to fill orders. Obviously, you don't want to order too much merchandise and end up with all your profits tied up in inventory if you cannot sell all your baskets by Valentine's Day. But you can alleviate this problem to some degree by ordering products that don't carry a specific Valentine's message, but instead have more generic messages like "Love" and "I Love You" written on them. These types of products you can eventually use for other occasions if they don't sell for Valentine's.

Before ordering any products from wholesale suppliers prior to a peak gift basket selling season, a realistic estimate must be calculated as to exactly how many basket orders your business can receive, and how many you can handle. If you start up as a home-based business, then obviously you won't get any last minute walk-in traffic like you would if you owned a retail gift basket store, so your business will come almost entirely from advance orders placed days or weeks before February 14th.

In order to motivate people to order early with your company, try using an "early bird" discount in your advertising and promotions. This will give people a five or ten percent discount if they order their basket three or four weeks before the actual holiday. With this much advance notice, ordering supplies will become much more predictable.

When these early orders start coming in, don't let them pile up unattended. If you have the supplies on hand, assemble and shrinkwrap the baskets and set them aside in your storage area. The more work you do ahead of time, the less last-minute rushing around you'll have to do as the holiday approaches. If you store the baskets for an extended period of time once they are wrapped, cover them with a sheet or light plactic drop cloth to keep the dust off the shrinkwrapping until they can be delivered to the customer.

Try to judge realistically just how many baskets you can assemble and deliver for a big day like Valentine's. Don't spend a lot of money on advertising unless you know you can recruit enough of your friends and family to help assemble the orders and deliver them on Valentine's Day. And, similarly, don't waste your promotional time and dollars to attract a huge number of orders if you are not sure you can order, and receive, all the supplies and ingredients needed for the basket orders. Remember, it's better to set a limit on the maximum amount of orders you can handle and stick to that limit, than to take on too many orders and not be able to deliver them by the promised date.

As the advance orders begin coming in for Valentine's, take up some of the slow time during the last week in January and the first week of February by adding decorations to the handles of baskets, making bows, and stuffing baskets with filler.

Since the majority of baskets will be personally delivered to the recipient, be very conservative on the number of deliveries that one person can handle for a day. One person can usually complete about ten to fifteen deliveries in an eight-hour day, provided that all the stops are within close proximity of each other. If a number of temporary workers will help out with the delivery, look at a street map of the city and determine the location of each of the delivery stops, then coordinate the drivers' routes so that each delivery person will follow the most efficient delivery path and schedule.

ORDER FORM

Date:_____   Salesperson:_____

Ordered By:_____   Deliver To:_____

_____   _____

_____   _____

Phone:_____   Phone:_____

Method of Delivery: __ Ship UPS __Personal Delivery __Customer Pick-Up

Items Ordered in Basket:	Cost Each

Total Basket Cost = _____

Sales Tax = _____

Shipping or Delivery Charge = _____

TOTAL DUE = _____

Method of Payment: ___VISA ___MC ___Am. Express ___Check ___Cash

Card No.:_____

Exp. Date:_____

Special Instructions or Messages: _____

_____

_____

_____

Date and Time to Make Delivery:_____

Actual Shipping Date:_____

JoAnn's Basket's, 123 Main St., Anytown, MI, 43251, (212) 555-1212

Sample order form. This gives you an idea of all the information you'll need to take with each order. If you like, xerox this form and put in your own company name at the bottom.

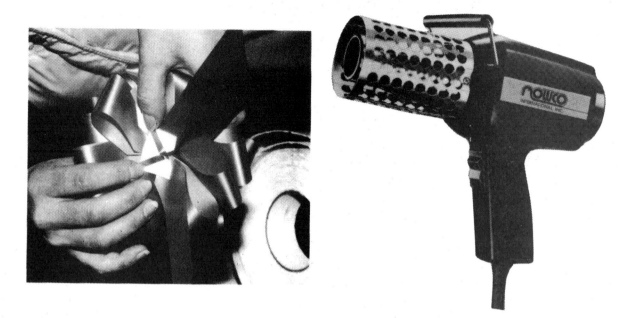

Many of the gift basket suppliers listed in the Supplier section of this manual sell products that make gift basket assembly easier, such as the double-sided stickers (left) used for sticking bows onto the baskets and the heavy-duty heat guns (right) for shrink-wrapping cellophane around the finished basket. (These are from Nowco International)

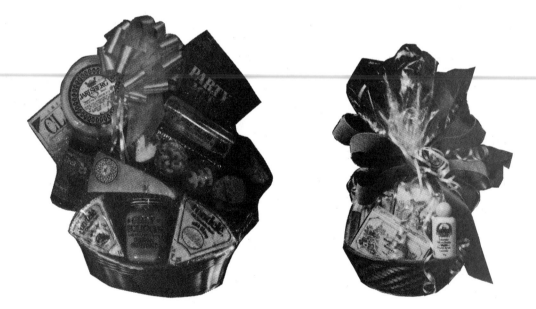

The basket shown on the left has been shrink-wrapped, while the one on the right uses a cellophane sheet tied at the top to hold the gifts in place. Shrink-wrapping offers the most secure and durable wrapping method for gift baskets that need to be shipped to the recipient.

Monthly Profit Potential

The following profit estimates are based upon two separate gift basket operations, one operating as a home-based business and the other set up in a retail commercial space. Both high and low-end estimates are given to show the potential range of profit and the correlation between increased sales and increased operating expenses. It should also be noted that these estimates take into account a gift basket business that has been operating for at least six months, so that initial start-up expenses have already been paid. Refer to the Start-Up section of this book for information on start-up expense projections.

Home-Based Gift Basket Business:

MONTHLY INCOME	Low	High
Gross Sales:	$3,000	$6,000
Minus Cost of Materials:	-1,500	-3,000
Gross Profit:	$1,500	$3,000
EXPENSES		
Advertising:	$200	$400
Phone:	50	100
Transportation:	40	80
Total Expenses:	$290	$580
NET PROFIT:	$1,210	$2,420

Retail Gift Basket Shop:

MONTHLY INCOME	Low	High
Gross Sales:	$8,000	$20,000
Minus Cost of Materials:	-3,000	-8,000
Gross Profit:	$5,000	$12,000

EXPENSES

	Low	High
Rent (800 square feet):	$400	$1,600
Payroll (1 to 3 part-timers):	1,000	3,000
Advertising:	500	1,000
Utilities/Phone:	300	600
Transportation:	100	500
Insurance:	150	250
Professional Services:	100	200
Total Expenses:	$2,550	$7,150
NET PROFIT:	**$2,450**	**$4,850**

Market

The Consumer Market

Almost everyone gives gifts at various times throughout the year; for birthdays, holidays, Christmas, etc. And gift baskets have enjoyed a boom in popularity because they are universal in their appeal and, as opposed to the traditional bouquet of flowers, offer reusable items that can be enjoyed for weeks after receiving the gift.

But as consumers have caught on to the benefits of gift baskets, the traditional retail outlets for this type of product, such as food markets and large gift boutiques, have been very slow to offer gift baskets for sale. According to many gift basket shop owners, this is because there is a good deal of thoughtful and detailed work needed to put together an attractive gift basket, and it's not something that large supermarkets and retailers are geared to handle. The result is that custom gift basket shops represent the best, and often only, place for consumers to go in search of quality gift baskets.

"The need for gift baskets arose because it's impossible to find them in supermarkets or other mass market stores except at Christmas time or Thanksgiving," says the owner of one gift basket retail store in California. "Also, it's hard to find fruit baskets and gourmet food baskets at the traditional gift or retail outlets," she adds, "and these are the most popular types of gift baskets."

At this point in time, women represent the majority of buyers who purchase most of the gift baskets sold through small gift basket shops, although the percentage of male gift basket purchasers is rising. Because these baskets come in such a wide price range, there is a corresponding wide range in the income and educational level of the typical buyer. As it stands right now, however, the consumer market for gift baskets primarily consists of middle and upper-middle class women.

Specifically, these are usually women in their 30's and 40's, mostly married with children and holding full-time jobs. These women have less time for shopping, so they're more inclined to pay someone else to make a gift basket for them, instead of trying to make their own. This market becomes very encouraging to prospective gift basket providers, when one considers that this represents the largest single block of consumers, in terms of average dollars spent each year on gifts.

You can also develop special markets within communities that have a high percentage of certain demographic segments of the population, such as college students or senior citizens. In you live in an area with large populations of these people, consider their gift giving, or gift receiving, needs, and how you might create baskets to help them.

The typical consumer will buy gifts for some, if not all, of the following occasions throughout the year:

Easter

birthdays

weddings and wedding showers

Christmas or Hanukkah

anniversaries

Thanksgiving

high school and college graduations

the birth of a child

Halloween

4th of July

New Year's

welcome home from vacations and trips

Valentine's Day

Mothers' Day and Fathers' Day

Secretarys' Day

Washington's Birthday (known for family visiting)

illness / get well presents

The Corporate Market

In the world of big business, or any size business for that matter, gift giving has become as intrinsic part of attracting and maintaining customers. This is not to say that customers choose to buy the products or services of one company over another based upon gifts they receive from these companies, but that small gifts are frequently given as a way of showing that one businessman appreciates the business of another. In fact, through the centuries gifts have been bestowed upon rulers and business acquaintances to reinforce relationships and create a favorable environment for business negotiations.

According to a study by the advertising faculty at the University of Florida, it's estimated that more than 50 million business gifts are distributed each year, for a total expenditure of over $1 billion. The vast majority of companies participating in this study stated that they felt their corporate gift giving programs to be effective promotional tools and planned to continue them in the future. The bottom line: it's always good business to let customers know that their patronage is appreciated.

According to one large gift basket franchisor, almost 30 to 40 percent of his company's total business comes from corporations who need to give business gifts. To develop this market, he has telemarketers call the person in charge of gift giving at these companies and send them a catalog of available ready-made gift baskets, a Rolodex-sized business card, and the phone number of his company's local affiliate store.

Christmas remains the most popular time for corporate gifts, but other occasions also require gifts, such as company anniversaries, Thanksgiving, and the individual birthdays of employees and clients. Milestone events in a company, such as a law firm winning a big case, or an architect finishing a large construction project, may also warrant gifts from these companies to their clients.

The majority of companies that practice executive gift giving don't have the time, the knowledge, or the personnel to shop and wrap the necessary gifts, so they must turn to either specialty advertising companies or custom gift basket marketers for help.

Put yourself in the shoes of the business client for a moment: If you run a large construction company with a number of clients, how do you go about shopping and finding gifts for each of these clients? It's much easier, and more professional, to hire a gift basket company to create and assemble a single type of basket that will appeal to these clients. The company giving the gift comes out ahead because they're presenting a gift custom-tailored to their clients without spending too much of their own time trying to shop for these gifts, and the recipient wins because he or she receives a gift that's thoughtful and probably a great deal more memorable than a traditional store-bought gift.

When planning your potential market within the corporate community keep in mind that the following businesses often give gifts to their clients and customers:

real estate offices and individual real estate agents

attorneys

doctors and dentists

insurance companies

architects and construction contractors

advertising agencies

graphic design studios

banks and mortgage companies

interior decorators

newspapers, radio and television stations

auto dealers

auto repair businesses

wholesale suppliers in any industry

Market Research

When compared to other service businesses, the gift basket business has the benefit of appealing to perhaps one of the broadest possible markets, but this is no excuse to avoid doing your homework and thoroughly investigating the potential customer base in the community. This planning will help you spend your advertising dollars more effectively and streamline your marketing efforts.

The primary consideration when researching your gift basket market is to find out who, if anyone, also provides gift baskets in your area, i.e. who will be your competition. Look through the Yellow Pages under "Gift Baskets" and "Baskets" to see if any companies already offer this service. Don't get discouraged if you find that other gift basket companies already exist because the potential market for this type of business is huge and most communities can provide enough business to keep a number of gift basket services profitable. Also remember that if you provide attractive baskets at a reasonable price you will develop a loyal following of repeat customers among your friends and family, all of whom undoubtedly give gifts throughout the year.

The next step in scouting the competition is to visit the many retail establishments that sell gift baskets and see what they offer. Check out supermarkets, gift and flower shops, gourmet food shops...even some liquor stores offer a limited selection of ready-made gourmet food and wine baskets. At each of these stores, note the ingredients in the baskets and the retail price they're asking. This knowledge will become very useful when it comes time to design some of your "standard" baskets and establish their selling price.

Also, check with your suppliers to see if they've heard of anyone else who's about to start a gift basket business in your area. For example, if you visit the wholesale gift mart (more about this in the Suppliers chapter) of the major metropolitan city near you to price some of the items you intend to buy wholesale, ask these wholesalers for their advice on your plans to start a gift basket company and inquire if they've run across anyone else from your market area who has similar plans.

Creating Your Own Market

The gift basket business traditionally revolves around very definite peak times of the year, such as Valentine's Day, Christmas, and Easter. But this leaves a long stretch of time during the summer without any big holidays. This means that a gift basket service has to come up with innovative ways to bring in a continual stream of business throughout the year. Apart from an aggressive advertising and promotional campaign, which is covered in the Advertising chapter of this book, new markets can be developed for each month of the year.

Customers will always need birthday and anniversary baskets throughout the year, but you can bring in more repeat business from the same customers every year by keeping all your customers on a file card system or, better yet, a computer. This way, you'll know when each customer has a birthday or anniversary coming up and can send out a reminder card or call them to see if they would like to buy another basket.

Another way to drum up more business is to think about the types of activities most people do at certain times of the year and create theme baskets accordingly. For example, during the summer, many people will go away on vacation, so you could contact travel agencies and sell them on the idea of sending bon voyage or thank you baskets to their clients who are just about to depart on their journey. Or, during football season in the fall, make baskets that husbands can give to their wives to appease them for spending so much time watching football games. "Tailgate" picnic baskets can also be popular gifts for people going to football games.

Gift baskets can be great gifts for parents and other relatives to send to kids who are away at boarding school or college. As much-appreciated "care packages," these baskets make great presents at any time during the school year, so don't forget to mention this to your customers who have children.

A worthwhile new idea developed by some gift basket services is to create a Basket-of-the-Month club and get people to sign up to buy one inexpensive gift basket every month, which they can send to their loved ones for birthdays or just as unexpected gifts. The type of baskets for this service would be in the $15 to $30 price range, plus the extra charge for shipping. It would be fairly cost-effective to run special advertisements to promote the basket-of-the-month concept, since just a few new customers to this service could pay for the cost of the ad over the course of the year.

Weddings usually take place in the spring, so this is another specific event you can focus on to attract new business as you head into the slower summer months. Try placing sample baskets in bridal shops, along with your business cards or brochures, to advertise your company to people planning weddings or buying bridesmaid dresses. As an incentive to the owners of these shops, offer to pay a commission of 10 or 20 percent of the retail price of any baskets sold as a result of the sample basket in their store. Or simply give the storekeeper the basket as a gift in exchange for letting you display it for a month or two.

This same strategy can be used in other retail stores and businesses: Many gift basket services have realized very good results from placing sample baskets in the waiting rooms of doctors and dentists offices, and also in lobbies of nursing homes. Other businesses are good bets too, as long as they have a steady stream of customers passing through who can notice the sample basket.

Other popular items to include in gift baskets include chocolates, seasonings, preserves, potpourri, wine, and custom-printed wine glasses or cups. To get a good idea of all that's available to you on a wholesale or retail basis, contact the suppliers listed in the manual and request their catalogues.

The Product

Every Basket Has a Theme

The key to marketing gift baskets is to develop a list of custom baskets created specifically for the occasions that most often require gifts, i.e. weddings, birthdays, anniversaries, etc. The most successful gift basket business owners put a great deal of time into developing new and attractive theme baskets, and use photo albums or printed flyers to show these baskets and their ingredients.

Maintaining such a selection of theme baskets will help the profitability of your business in two important ways. First, if you design a number of theme baskets and find that some of them have ingredients in common, such as a type of gourmet cheese or wine, you can buy these ingredients in bulk from a wholesale supplier and increase your profit margin on the baskets that use these ingredients.

Secondly, if you can show customers the catalog or photo album of theme baskets, they will often pick from one of the designs instead of ordering a completely custom-built basket. Thus, when they order a pre-designed theme basket, you will increase your likelyhood of selling them a basket comprised of ingredients you bought for wholesale prices, rather than assembling a completely custom basket from ingredients that cost you the full retail price. Consequently, you'll enjoy a greater profit margin on these baskets.

Following are the names and contents of some popular theme baskets. These should act as a starting point for your own creative efforts and give you an idea of what customers like to have included in their gift baskets:

Anniversary: A basket filled with chocolates, candies, and champagne. Custom-engraved champagne glasses also add a nice touch to this basket, if the customer is willing to pay the extra $10 to $20 that you'll have to charge for the engraving, which you can have done by an engraver.

Bachelor Party: Carrying the spirit of the bachelor party, this gift basket offers such items as a six-pack of imported beer, garters, beer mugs, and noise makers.

Beach Blanket Bingo: Everything needed for a beach barbeque: small, 12-inch tabletop grill, barbeque mitt, tongs, basting brush barbeque sauce, mustard and catsup bottles.

Bon Voyage: Designed to be given to a friend or loved one about to embark on a vacation, this basket offers such traveller's necessities as: maps, translation books, suntan lotion, a good novel to read on the plane flight, etc.

The Bridal Basket: This is a standard basket in every gift basket shop and you should create your own variation using bridal gifts like lace garters, small picture frames, linen hankerchiefs, "his and her" champagne glasses, photo albums, and other wedding-related items.

Chocolate Lover's Paradise: A gold tin full of gourmet chocolate bars and chocolate animals, chocolate-covered almonds and walnuts, and cocoa mixes.

Clambake: Amidst a basket draped in pieces of old fishnet and decorated with seashells sits tins of gourmet choppped clams, horseradish mustard, and seafood butter.

Down on the Farm: An assortment of jellies, jams, nuts, and cheeses, resting on checkered napkins. A bottle of wine also adds a nice touch to this basket.

Fiesta in a Basket: This hacienda helper features Cuervo Gold Tequila, Margarita Mix, Triple Sec, and margarita salt, plus an ample supply of blue corn chips and salsa.

For Her Eyes Only: A delicate, feminine basket for the special lady in someone's life. Trimmed in ribbons and roses, this basket features preserves, honeys, breakfast teas, floral-patterned photo frames, and a small diary. Lingerie can also be added.

For Men Only: A macho basket of rare imported beer, smoked meats and salmon, roasted nuts, pretzels, and other munchies to go with the beer. A beer stein can also add to this theme.

The Fruits of Success: A mountain of fresh fruit piled high in the basket and garnished with selected nuts and holiday candies.

Golden Years: A basket tailored for birthdays in the high double digits. This assortment includes humorous gifts like personalized mugs, coffee cups, balloons, etc. , in addition to engraved wine glasses.

Gourmet's Choice: A standard in the gift basket industry, this type of basket features a custom arrangement for the connoisseur of fine foods, such as imported wine, cheeses, pate, Dijon mustard, pecan apple butter, smoked Alaskan salmon, imported coffees and teas, and cloth napkins.

Gourmet Kitchen Mitt: Use a large, colorful cooking mitt and fill it with quality cooking utensils, such as wooden spoons, or knives, and add cloth kitchen towels and bottles of herbs.

Happy Hanukkah: Incorporating fine kosher wines, like Baron Jaquab de Herzog Chenin Blanc and Hagafen Pinot, this Hanukkah basket will lift someone's spirits during the holdiday season. Also include kosher crackers and snacks.

Hawaiian Holiday: A tropical blend of macadamia nuts, Hawaiian bread, Kona coffees, kiwi fruit, and kiwi salad dressing. Trimmed with colorful bird of paradise flowers or exotic silk flowers.

Holiday Greetings: A mixture of potpourri, scented candles, fragrence sprays, gourmet coffees, and jelly cookies.

Lifestyles of the Rich and Famous: A basket for the millionaire-to-be, this gift features champagne and champagne glasses, caviar with a silver spoon, monogrammed cloth napkins, and gourmet crackers and cheese.

Say Cheese: A single bottle of white Bordeaux wine surrounded by a wide assortment of imported gourmet cheeses. Salami, pate', and crackers complete the feast.

Secretary's Treat: A gift of appreciation for a secretary or co-worker. This basket could offer chocolates, jelly-filled cookies, gift certificates, and a bottle of wine.

Southwestern Surprise: An assortment of cactus salsa, bar-b-que sauce, blue corn tortilla chips, spicy bean dip, chili powder, and other southwestern food specialties, all packed in a rugged, desert-colored basket. Larger versions of this basket could include margarita mix, limes, and margarita glasses.

Sparkling Celebration: A white willow basket overflowing with elegant surprises. Two bottles of champagne, chocolate truffles, imported caviar, seafood pate', and imported gourmet cheeses.

Special Lady: For a special woman, whether it's a mother, wife, or any other loved one. This basket includes scented bath soaps, bubble bath, skin cremes, bath beads, and other pampering products.

Sunrise Surprise: A beautiful basket full of breakfast goodies. Delicacies include Jamaican Blue Mountain coffee, imported teas, cocoa, Irish Oatmeal, wild honey, Five Grain Pancake mix, and bisquits.

Your Cup of Tea: A basket for the tea lover. An elegant ensemble of premium teas arranged with a serving tray, teapot, cloth napkins, scone mix, jelly, jam, pickled oranges, and tea cake.

Viva Italia: An Italian theme basket complete with different varieties of gourmet pasta (such as spinich and basil flavored noodles), a block of parmesian cheese, extra virgin olive oil, a jar of olives, large pasta fork, and cloth napkins. Larger versions of this basket could also include a bottle of Italian wine and wine glasses.

Expanded Profits with Balloons

Once your gift basket service is up and running, you might want to branch out and offer the additional service of balloon delivery. Because of the the popularity of balloons as gift supplements, the majority of successful gift basket stores provide balloon arrangements as an added profit center to their business.

"Balloons call attention to the act of gift giving and turn it into more of an event, especially when the gift and balloons are delivered personally by a messenger," says Joe DelVecchio of Balloon Bouquets, a national balloon delivery franchise based in Washington, DC. DelVecchio's company offers balloon deliveries for prices that range from $20 to $50. A standard fee of $32.50 gets customers a gift package of six balloons and a gift item, such as a bottle of champagne or chocolates.

Balloon Bouquets operates a national sales office that runs national advertisements to attract customers, then refers these customers to the local Balloon Bouquet affiliate store near their local area. They emphasize the fact that their balloon arrangements are delivered by a live person, and not just shipped to the gift recipient. Often these delivery people wear tuxedos and work hard to develop their showmanship when making personal deliveries.

Most gift basket services that offer balloons use latex balloons filled with helium. On large orders, such as a corporate event or theme party where hundreds of balloons are needed, a customized message is sometimes ordered by the customer to be printed on the balloons.

Gift Wrapping Inside Balloons

One innovative way to make gift baskets truly unique is to place small gift items inside of inflated balloons, a feat that is made possible by a special vacuum-inflation device created by Balloon Wrap of Yorba Linda, California.

"Our machine really attracts attention because it enables you to put anything in an inflated balloon—flowers, jewelry, clothing items, stuffed animals, dolls, etc.—as long as it doesn't have any sharp edges on it," says company founder and president Les Wigger.

The concept behind the balloon wrapping machine is simple: the uninflated balloon attaches to a 4-inch diameter tube inside an air-tight vacuum chamber. When the air inside the chamber gets pumped out, the normal air pressure in the room flows down into the balloon and expands it out. Once the balloon is in the fully-inflated position, the gift can be dropped down through the tube into the balloon. The customer usually pays from $3 to $5 for this wrapping service, if he provides the gift item himself.

By incorporating these balloon-wrapped gifts in your gift baskets, you can charge more for the basket and increase your profit margin, or use the added service as a way to generate more business for the gift basket service. Also, gift-filled balloons can be shipped along with gift baskets to a recipient in another city or state. Since the balloons stay inflated for two to three weeks, they won't deflate by the time they arrive at their destination.

"When I first started as a balloon wrap dealer, we set up a few sample balloons in the lobbies of busy office buildings, and the rush was on," says one Balloon Wrap dealer in Los Angeles. He grossed $600 during his first week in business, largely by taking orders phoned in to him from people who had seen his Balloon Wrap display in their office building.

The Balloon Wrap dealership sells for $1,495, which includes the balloon inflating machine, an assortment of balloons, advertising materials, and assistance in operations and marketing the business. This start-up package also includes six hours of instructional videotape that shows how to use the balloon wrapping machines and how to promote it to potential customers.

If this start-up costs seems like too steep of an investment for a new gift basket service, consider locating a Balloon Wrap dealer in your local area who could perhaps work with you and provide balloon gift wrapping services at a low volume discount if you bring a minimum number of jobs to him each month.

For more information, contact Balloon Wrap at: 3940-F Prospect Ave., Yorba Linda, CA 92686, (714) 993-2295.

Additional Products

If you set up your gift basket business in a retail shop, you'll quickly find additional profit centers available by selling various gift-related items that don't necessarily go into your gift baskets. Such add-ons as greeting cards, novelty gifts, stickers, gift-wrapping supplies, etc. have been sold successfully at many gift basket shops. It should be noted, however, that this merchandise is usually sold by gift basket services that operate out of retail storefronts, since customers tend to buy most of these items on impulse.

To find ideas for additional gift items you can sell, look through the gift industry magazines listed in the Appendix section at the back of this book and visit the manufacturer showrooms in the "gift mart" near you. You'll find a list of these marts in the Supplier section of this book.

The photo above shows how to use the packing grass and paper to build a base within the basket before starting to stack the gift items. You can use foil-covered boxes, such as the one shown below, as attractive containers for low-priced gift basket creations. (Both the custom-printed packing paper shown above and the foil boxes are available from Nowco International.)

Creating the Gift Baskets

Your skill as a gift basket artist will come about from practice on your own baskets and from studying the baskets of your competitors. Once you've made a few baskets, you'll feel more confident about developing original designs and experimenting with decorations and accessories.

The basic basket assembly process is simple: First, take the empty basket and the items to include in it and lay them out on the work table. Visualize the finished basket, with the assorted items arranged inside and one or two main items positioned at the top as centerpieces.

Line the bottom of the basket with tissue paper up to the rim. If you want to save on shredded paper "grass," use brown butcher paper folded up so that it takes up the bulk of the space at the bottom of the basket. Some suppliers (such as Nowco) also offer brown packing paper that's printed to look like an old Victorian newspaper, with articles on food, wine, coffee, and many other gourmet trivia items that makes the bottom of the basket look more interesting than when it's filled with plain brown packing paper.

Regular newspaper can also be used at the bottom of the basket as a base. If you don't like the appearance of newspaper, but want to use it as a cost-saving measure, then try wrapping the folded-up wad of newspaper with a layer of gift-wrapping paper or plain brown "butcher" paper before placing it at the bottom of the basket.

Next, put in a layer of shredded paper grass along the bottom. On top of this layer set the first level of gift products, arranging them in a circle with each product leaning in toward the center slightly. If necessary, use clear tape to secure the bottom of these items to the basket or to each other, so they don't move around too much once the basket is complete. (A 10-pound box of shredded paper grass should be sufficient to fill from 15 to 20 baskets.)

After this, add more shredded paper and place the second level of gift items in the basket, arranging them in a smaller circle inside the first layer of gifts. This top level should tilt inward at more of angle than the bottom level. Adjust the shredded paper to support these items and add a third, smaller circle of gifts on top if room permits. On top of all these items, place the main centerpiece gift and fill the remaining space with more shredded paper.

Once all the items have been placed in the basket, cut a piece of cellophane large enough to cover the basket and extend far off over its sides. Lay the cellophane down on the table and set the basket on top of it. Pull up the cellophane around the basket and gather it together at the top of the basket. Use a bow to tie the cellophane at this point and attach a blank greeting card and envelope to the bow. If you have any labels with your company name, stick one at the center of the cellophane covering. Ribbons, garnish, and bows give your packaging an added dimension of quality and craftmanship at a very small extra cost, so it's worthwhile to put some thought into adding these accessories to the basket handle and the outside of the basket.

Once the basket is finished, tape the customer's order form/sales receipt to it and set it aside for the customer to pick up or to be delivered later. After some practice, you should be able to complete 7 to 14 baskets each afternoon.

Shrink Wrapping the Basket

Shrink wrapping is an alternative to using cellophane. Some of the companies listed in the Supplier chapter of this book sell shrink wrapping kits that you can use to cover the baskets with a more tightly fitting layer of "shrink film". Most of these shrink wrapping systems sell for $100 to $300 and consist of basically a shrink film roll dispenser and a high-powered heat gun (similar to a blow dryer for your hair) that blows hot air onto the plastic and causes it to shrink up tightly around the gift items in the basket.

The main advantage of the shrink wrapper is that it allows gift items to be stacked up higher in the basket, since they are held in place more securely by the shrunken plastic wrapping, and this gives more of an impression that the basket is just bursting with goodies. It also provides a more robust wrapping system for baskets that are shipped to the recipient, rather than hand delivered.

The shrink wrapping gun is easy to use after a little bit of practice. First cut out a sheet of shrink film and drap it over the top of the basket, so that the excess film is taken up at the back of the basket and taped together with clear tape. With the heat gun held four to six inches away from the back of the basket, quickly move the gun across the film in strokes, as if you were using a spray paint gun. It's best to start applying the hot air in the back of the basket at the bottom, then work around to the front. Be careful not to hold the heat gun too close to the film, or hold it on any one spot continuously, since this will burn a hole in the plastic and you'll have to start the whole thing over again.

Once you've shrunken the film on the back side of the basket to take up the slack in the shrink film, move to the front and brush the heat gun across the film in smooth, continuous strokes. As you do this, you'll see the film tighten up and become smooth. Any loose spots can be tightened up by a very quick blast from the heat gun. The entire heat shrinking process should only take from one to two minutes, once you get the hang of it.

One of the problems with shrink wrapping is that you often end up with a big mound of shrink film taped at the back of the basket, which can hurt the aesthetic appeal of the gift. To alleviate this problem, Nowco (listed in Supplier chapter) has developed a special shrink wrapping system that removes all the excess shrink film and provides a much "cleaner" looking shrink wrap to the basket.

With the Nowco system, the shrink film is first draped over the basket so that one half of the film hangs over the front of the basket and the other half of the film sheet hangs over the back of the basket. Next, a special "heat sealer" gun (which looks like a small clamp) clamps off and melts together the two front and back sides of the film to form a seam that follows the contour of the basket. Once this is done, the excess film on the outside of this seam is cut off and discarded, leaving a bag-like film coverring that fits loosely over the basket. A regular heat gun is then applied to this film bag to shrink wrap it around the gift items in the basket. The result is a perfectly-fitting plastic film without any of the overlapping excess plastic produced by normal shrink wrap systems.

Your shrink wrapping system can start out small, with just a heat gun and a roll of plastic film, and expand in accordance to increasing business volume. The heat gun will work well for gift basket services that shrink wrap an average of up to five baskets a day. As volume increases beyond this point, the next step would be to buy a hand-held heat sealer. If the number of gift baskets needing to be shrink wrapped reaches a level of over 20 or 30 a day, then it would be time to consider investing in a complete shrink wrapping table, with built in roller for the shrink film and a large heater/cutter unit. These industrial-grade tables can run anywhere from $500 to over $1,000 in price. When buying the shrink wrap film, expect to pay around $20 to $25 for a 100-foot roll and about $70 to $80 for a 500-foot roll.

Make Your Baskets Colorful

In addition to the shape of the basket itself and the gift items inside the basket, the color of the ribbons, straw filler, and other trimmings creates a large part of the basket's appeal and beauty. As you grow more confident in your basket making skills begin to experiment with brighter colors and venture out beyond the traditional pinks and powder blue colors of most gift baskets.

Using certain colors will help accent specific basket themes. Green, for example, has obvious uses in baskets made for Christmas and St. Patrick's Day. But this color also connotes feelings of peace and tranquility, and therefore can be used for gifts that someone would buy for another member of their family, for example, or for "get-well" presents.

Red, on the other hand, conveys excitement and passion. This color stirs human emotions and is most often used for Valentine's Day baskets and baskets for other romantic occasions. Pink is a toned-down version of red, and therefore isn't as powerful. Pink is also an emotional color, but presents more of an affectionate, rather than passionate, mood. Pinks are good, therefore, for Mother's Day baskets, as well as Valentine's Day gifts.

Although light blue is definitely the color of choice for baby baskets intended for little boys, darker blues can be a great color for gift baskets geared toward adult males. Deep indigo blue represents stability and nobility, good tones for corporate baskets aimed at corporate executives, or even baskets given as gifts of condolence.

Violet is a mixture of blue and red, and is the color of mystery and dreams, and is therefore useful for gift baskets incorporating metaphysical gifts.

Yellow is the best color for conveying a sense of cheerfulness and optimism. It's sense of clean, enlightened emotions means it is a great color to accent get well baskets and also baby baskets. As a variation of yellow, orange carries a more down-to-earth feeling of vibrancy and is often overlooked in gift basket designs outside of Holloween. A mixture of red and yellow, orange is a high-energy color and can add a sense of energy to romantic-themed baskets, baby baskets, and even as a subtle accent color to dark-blue themed corporate baskets.

When mixing colors together in decorating a basket, keep in mind that some colors complement others, and therefore can be used together for a visually pleasing effect. Here are the primary complementary color combinations:

- red and green
- blue and orange
- violet and yellow

If a combination of three colors is needed, the following groupings complement each other:

- red, yellow, blue
- green, violet, orange

Colors can also be divided into "warm" and "cool" variations. These designations can be helpful if you want to use warm colors to accent a predominantly cool-colored basket, or visa-versa. The basic warm colors are yellow, red, orange, and light green (since it has traces of yellow in it). Cool colors include purple, all shades of blue, and darker greens.

Another way to approach color coordination is to take one basic color and accent it with complementary colors that have varying traces of that primary color in them.

For example, if the basic color is yellow, then use accents of orange and red, since these two colors have yellow in them. For a basic color of blue, try using greens and even yellow as complementary accents. For a red basic color, use accents of violet and blue.

Staining Baskets

Although most baskets will be used in the exact same condition as they are bought, an application of stain or paint can transform a dull or plain looking basket into a rich and colorful gift container. Standard wood stain, which comes in a variety of colors, works very well for this process.

To get started, lay out many layers of newspaper on top of the workbench and make sure to wear rubber gloves at all times. Since most baskets presents a rough and eneven surface, it's usually quicker and easier to use a paint brush to apply the stain, rather than a rag. Most average-sized baskets will require about a half pint of stain to cover both the outside and inside surfaces with one good coat.

While applying the stain to the basket, turn it around continously to make sure that every part of it is evenly covered with stain. Although most baskets will require only one coat of stain, a darker Mahogany look can be achieved by adding a second coat after allowing the first coat to dry for a period of 24 hours.

Wood baskets can also be greatly enhanced by a coat of bright paint, which can be either brushed on or sprayed. When brushing on a high-gloss enamel paint, a single coat is usually all that's needed in most cases. Use a small regular paint brush and slowly turn the basket as you apply the paint, making sure to cover all the surface areas, including the inside and bottom of the basket.

Spray painting requires a little bit more skill and patience, since care must be taken to make sure the paint is applied evenly. Use light, steady strokes when spraying the paint, and continue with the stroke past the end of the basket surface so that a puddle of paint doesn't build up at the end point of each stroke. With most colors, a second, and even third coat of paint will be needed, but it's best to let each coat dry for a few hours before applying the second coat. And, as with brushing on the paint, make sure to turn the basket while painting to cover all of its surfaces.

As an finishing touch to add over either the stain or paint, try a few coats of clear gloss finish. This will give the basket's finish a deep, rich appearance. When spraying on this clear finish, use light strokes and let it dry thoroughly between coats. After the final coat has been applied let the basket dry, then inspect it for any flat spots where the finish isn't glossy. Touch up these spots with a light coat.

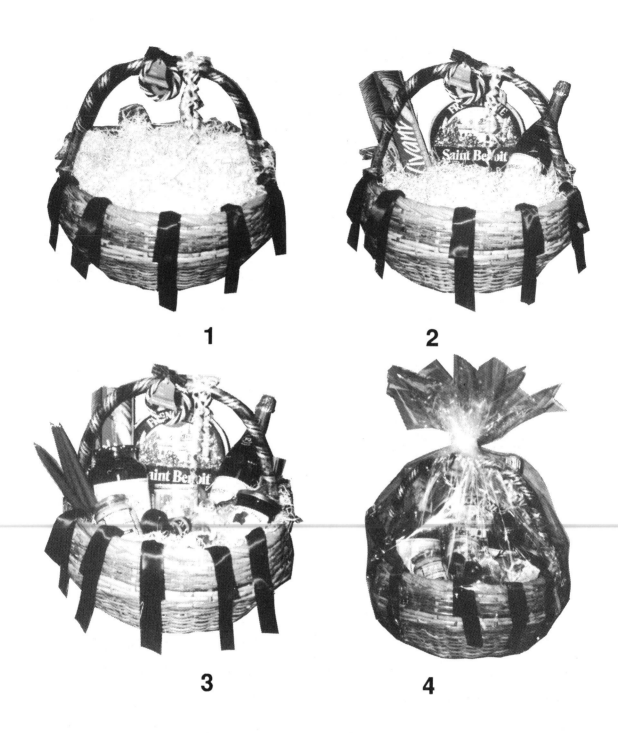

1   **2**

3   **4**

These photos show a gift basket in various stages of assembly. First (1) the empty basket is filled with shredded paper to form a base and ribbons are draped over the front of the basket. Next (2), the larger items are placed in the back of the basket. Following this (3), smaller items are placed in the front, with consideration given to the weight of each of the items, so that the finished basket is balanced when held by the handle. As the final step (4), the cellophane wrapping is placed under the basket and brought up to be tied at the top of the handle.

Buying Supplies Wholesale

Although many of the items in one-of-a-kind custom gift baskets will have to be purchased from the local supermarket at the full retail price, you can buy some frequently-used items in bulk for a wholesale price. This will add significantly to the profit margin on the baskets, since wholesale prices can often be 40% to 60% off the retail price. For example, a basket that would sell for a retail price of $5.00 from a local hardware store might only cost $3.00 each when purchased from a wholesaler. With the wholesaler, however, you will usually have to order a certain minimum amount of baskets with each order. So, refrain from buying anything wholesale until you've experimented with a line of "standard," ready-made baskets and know exactly what ingredients will be needed.

When contacting suppliers the first time, expect to fill out a credit application even if you're paying cash for the order. Many wholesalers require this information on all their new accounts, so don't be offended or surprised. The credit application will ask for your business savings and checking account numbers and the bank branch. It will also ask for trade references, which are companies you're already done business with on credit. Never try to inflate any figures on your bank account balances or accounts receivable, as the majority of suppliers will call to verify the information on the credit application.

And don't despair if you're just starting out with a small home-based business and don't have any trade references. As an alternative, you can ask the supplier if he or she will accept a personal credit reference instead. The bottom line is that you must show you're a dependable businessperson who will pay your bills on time.

Most of the time, wholesalers will put new accounts on a "C.O.D.", or prepayment, basis for their first few orders, which means that you must send a check along with the order, rather than receive the goods on credit. Don't argue about this—it's standard practice and isn't intended as a personal insult. After a few orders, the supplier will usually begin extending credit, so be patient.

Once you're on credit terms with a supplier, you will usually be asked to pay invoices within 30 days of receiving them. This is called a "net 30" credit arrangement. Many companies offer a small discount of 2 percent off the bill if it's paid within 10 days. On large orders, these discounts can add up to a significant savings, so don't forget to take advantage of this if you have the cash on hand to pay off the invoice early.

Don't forget to always calculate freight and shipping charges when ordering goods that have to be shipped to you. With bulky items, such as baskets and some food products, the shipping charges can become very expensive, so make sure to find these out when placing the order.

Gift Buyers' Marts

Almost every major metropolitan city has a giftware "mart," which is a building where reps from each of the large giftware manufacturers maintain an office/ showroom to service local retail accounts such as gift shops and gift basket companies. Visit the mart nearest you and spend a day walking from showroom to showroom, examining the lastest gift products for sale, since many of these items can be incorporated into gift basket designs. Here is a list of the marts in many of the large cities across the country:

Atlanta Merchandise Mart
240 Peachtree St. N.W., Atlanta, GA 30043, (404) 688-8994

The Center
59 Middlesex Turnpike, Bedford, MA 01730, (617) 275-2775

Charlotte Merchandise Mart
2500 E. Independence Blvd., Charlotte, NC 28205, (704) 377-5881

Columbus Gift Mart
1999 Westbelt Dr., Columbus, OH 43228, (614) 876-2719

Dallas Market Center

2100 Stemmons Freeway, Dallas, TX 75207, (214) 655-6100

Denver Merchandise Mart

451 E. 58th Ave., Denver, CO 80216, (303) 292-6278

Design Center Northwest

5701 Sixth Avenue South, Seattle, WA 98108, (206) 762-1200

Gift Center at Montgomery Park

2701 N.W. Vaughn St., Portland, OR 97210, (503) 228-7275

Indianapolis Gift Mart

4475 Allisonville Road, Indianapolis, IN 46205, (317) 546-0719

International Home Furnishings Center

210 E. Commerce St., High Point, NC 27260, (919) 889-6144

Kansas City Merchandise Mart

6800 W. 115th St., Overland Park, KS 66211, (913) 491-6688.

Los Angeles Mart

1933 South Broadway, Los Angeles, CA 90007, (213) 749-7911

Marketcenter

230 Fifth Avenue, New York, NY 10001, (212) 512-9555

The Merchandise Mart

Merchandise Mart Plaza, Chicago, IL 60654, (312) 527-4141

Miami International Merchandise Mart

777 N.W. 72nd Ave., Miami, FL 33126, (305) 261-2900

Michigan Association of Gift Salesmen

133 W. Main Street, Northville Square, Northville, MI 48167, (313) 348-7890

Mid-Atlantic Gift Center

12260 Sunrise Valley Dr., Reston, VA 22091, (703) 391-0095

Minneapolis Gift Mart

10301 Bren Rd. West, Minnetonka, MN 55343, (612) 932-7200

New York Merchandise Mart

41 Madison Ave., New York, NY 10010, (212) 686-1203

The Pittsburgh Expo Mart

105 Mall Boulevard, Monroeville, PA 15146, (412) 856-8100

San Francisco Giftcenter

888 Brannan Street, San Francisco, CA 94103, (415) 861-7733

Seattle Gift Mart

6100 Fourth Ave. South, Seattle, WA 98108, (206) 767-6800

Western Merchandise Mart

1355 Market St., San Francisco, CA, 94103, (415) 552-2311

Suppliers

The first supplier to line up is for the baskets themselves. Try to find a local supplier for these because they will often be needed on short notice. To find local basket wholesalers, look in the Yellow Pages under "Baskets" and visit the nearest wholesale gift buyer's mart. Also, ask around at nearby florist shops and gift stores to see if the managers of these businesses know where to buy wholesale baskets in the local market.

The following list represents many of the biggest wholesale suppliers in the gift industry. While this list does not mention all the suppliers in this business, it offers a good base for further research. When you see a supplier that sells items you might be interested in purchasing in bulk for the wholesale price (usually around 40% to 50% of the retail price), call or write the company mentioned and request a catalog and wholesale price list.

ACC Company, 1150 Broadway / P.O. Box 118, Hewlett, NY 11557, (519) 569-1300 (crystal gift items)

American Cooking Guild, 2915 Fenimore Road / Box 2691, Silver Spring, MD 20902 (cookbooks)

American Vintage Wine Bisquits, 70-A Greenwich Ave., Suite 165, New York, NY 10011 (718) 361-1003 (low cholesterol handmade bisquits)

American Wicker and Wood Mfg. Company, Highway 67, P.O. Box 75, Mountain City, TN 37683 (baskets)

Ande Rooney, P.O. Box 758, Port Ewen, NY 12466, (914) 339-5533

Aromax Inc., P.O. Box 3068, Visalia, CA 93278, (800) 344-7286 (potpourri, candles, incense)

Artifacts Inc., P.O. Box 3399, Palestine, TX 75802, (214) 729-4178 (candles)

Basket Supply Center, Inc., 2320 Irving Blvd., Dallas, TX 75207, (214) 263-7292 (wide assortment of natural-colored and stained baskets)

The Basket Works, The Dickey Mill, 4900 Wetheredsville Road, Baltimore, MD 21207 (tools, dyes, and kits for weaving baskets)

Basketville Inc., Main St. Box 710, Putney, VT 05346 (baskets)

Biedermann & Sons, 162 Northfield Road, Northfield, IL 60093, (312) 446-8150 (candles)

Birin Chocolates, Cleveland & Madison Avenues, Highland Park, NJ 08904, (908) 545-4400 (chocolate truffles, boxed or in bulk)

Bitterman's Confections, 1625 Oak St., Kansas City, MO 64108 (chocolates, candies)

Blind Made Prods./Services for the Blind, 5310-A Fayetteville Rd., Raleigh, NC 27603 (baskets)

Brooklyn Bow & Ribbon Company, 150 Denton Ave. / P.O. Box 508, Lynbrook, NY 11563, (516) 887-4600 (bows and ribbons for gift basket wrapping)

Brown Bag Cookie Art, Box F, Hill, NH 03243, (800) 228-4488 (custom ceramic cookie molds)

The Bug House, 306 E. 12th Street #300, Kansas City, MO 64106, (816) 472-8585 (china miniatures)

Carolina Basket and Wood Works, P.O. Box 1418, Columbia, SC 29202 (baskets)

Carolina Designs, Ltd., P.O. Box 2806, Oshkosh, WI 54903, (800) 654-5271 (bath and home fragrance gifts)

Cella's Sweets, P.O. Box 424, Grand Ledge, MI 48837 (517) 627-1910 (custom-packaged wafer cookies)

Chandler Press, Box 268, Maynard, MA 01754, (small nineteenth century gift books on cookery, games, railroading, etc.)

Christopher Brooks Distinctive Foods, 3006 29th St. S.W., Suite F, Tumwater, WA 98502, (206) 352-5051 (over 100 products for gift basket makers, such as teas, marmalades, crackers, and liquid herbs)

Coast Wholesale Florists, 149 Morris Street, San Francisco, CA 94107 (baskets)

Coe & Dru Trade Company, 6250 Boyle Ave., Vernon, CA 90058, (213) 582-2550 (picnic baskets)

Coffee Express Co., 1342 N. Main, Ann Arbor, MI 48104, (313) 769-2040 (wide variety of straight, blended, decaffeinated, and flavored coffees)

Comoy's of London, 65-10 69th Place, Queens, NY 11379, (718) 326-2233 (scrimshaw carvings in reproduction ivory)

Contessa Manufacturing Inc., 2400 Marcus Ave., New Hyde Park, NY 11042 (baskets)

Country Mixes, Box 1130, Dublin, OH 43017, (herb mixes)

Creative Arts Flowers, 85 Commerce Drive, Hauppauge, NY 11788 (bridal accessories, silk flowers, Christmas decorations)

Creative Concepts, 2018 Riverside Drive, Danville, VA 24540 (800) 782-8809 (jelly beans packaged in sundae jars and bottles)

Creative Cookie Company, 3900 16th St. N.W., Washington, DC 20011, (202) 722-1048 (holiday and special occasion fortune cookies)

CTI Industries, Barrington, IL 60010 (manufacturers of a full line of themed message balloons for Mother's Day, Father's Day, and many other occassions)

David M & Company, 6029 Etiwanda Ave., Tarzana, CA 91356, (818) 705-0941 (greeting cards)

Davidson's, P.O. Box 11214, Reno, NV 89510 (702) 356-1690 (flavored teas, jams, and gift specialty items for gift baskets)

DMS Treasures, Haverhill, MA 01830, (508) 373-9106 (potpourri)

Ernex Corporation, 2262 Bath Ave., Brooklyn, NY 11214, (718) 449-7555 (custom molded chocolate sculptures)

Excelsior Incense Works, 1413 Van Dyke Avenue, San Francisco, CA 94124, (415) 822-9123 (potpourris, scented candles, incense, bath salts)

Fairwinds Gourmet Coffee, Concord, NH, (800) 645-4515 (gourmet coffee in 8oz. gift-size packages)

Flemat Company, P.O. Box 245, Pacific Grove, CA 93950, (408) 372-2918 (ornaments, nutcrackers, toys, advent calendars)

Foley-Martens Company, 3300 N.E. 5th St. Minneapolis, MN 55418 (baskets)

Four Seasons Shredding Company, 2266 N. Prospect Ave., Milwaukee, WI 53203 (414) 271-4340 (bio-degradable fine shredded packing material in assorted colors and textures)

Gaylord Specialties Corp., 225 Fifth Ave. #445, New York, NY 10010, (212) 683-6182 (shopping bags, ribbons, bows, wraping tissue, labels)

Gift Basket Supplies, Inc., 65 North Main Street, Brockton, MA 02401, (800) 227-5381 (supplier of bag-shaped shrink wrapping film and over 2000 various packaging products)

Gift Basket Supply World, 1830 Air Lane Drive, Suite 5, Nashville, TN 37210, (800) 786-4438 (baskets, wrapping material, and wide selection of specialty gift items)

Gifts International & Fulfillment Services, Inc., P.O. Box 1749, Maryland Heights, MO 63043 (714) 832-7884 (large selection of over 200 pre-packaged gift items)

Glerup-Revere, P.O. Box 15770, Seattle, WA 98115, (206) 523-4203 (small gift boxes, decorative cellophane bags, and tissues)

Golden Walnut Cookie Company, 3840 Swanson Court, Gurnee, IL 60031, (708) 244-8050 (almond ingot cakes and individual cookies wrapped in clear film)

Grandma Pfeiffer's Inc., P.O. Box 1627, Lake Oswego, OR 97035, (800) 446-8574 (gift cakes baked in a jar and topped with laced lids)

Great Northwestern Greeting Seed Company, P.O. Box 776, Oregon City, OR

97045, (503) 631-3425 (greeting cards filled with seeds, teas, herbs, & bubble bath)

Harper-Lee International, P.O. Box 279, Roan Mountain, TN 37687, (615) 772-3233 (perfume bottles, atomizers, paper weights)

Harry London Candies, 1281 S. Main Street, North Canton, OH 44720, (216) 494-2757 (chocolate gift items)

Heartland Samplers, Inc., 9947 Valley View Rd., Eden Prairie, MN 55344 (inspirational gift calendars)

Hill's Imports, Inc., West Coast Shipping: 31908 Hayman Street, Hayward, CA 94544, (415) 471-2896. East Coast Shipping: 602 South 10th Street, Allentown, PA 18103, (215) 776-1488. (importer of over 1,000 varieties of baskets)

The Jack Company, 8403 Garden Gate Place, Boca Raton, FL 33433 (407) 479-2629 (champagne bottled gourmet popcorn, chocolate gourmet jelly beans, assorted flavor gourmet jelly beans)

Jacquard Francaise, 200 Lover's Lane, Culpepper, VA 22710, (linens)

Jamie Lynn, 6445 W. Grand Ave., Chicago, IL 60635, (312) 622-6445 (bridal accessories, memory books, garters, champagne glasses, desk pens)

Jetram Sales, Inc., 1611 Manufacturers Dr., Fenton, MO 63026 (314) 343-9585 (suppliers of shrink wrapping equipment specifically designed for gift baskets)

Julia's Own, 307 North Avenue, Barrington, IL 60010, (708) 382-4536 (scented gift sachets)

Kensington Cards, 2210 Wilshire Blvd. #627, Santa Monica, CA 90403, (213) 398-

6036 (fine art greeting cards from England)

Koppers Chocolate Specialty Co., Inc., New York, NY (212) 243-0220 (manufactuer of gourmet gift confections, such as chocolates and jelly beans)

Kozlowski Farms, 5566 Gravenstein Hwy., Forestville, CA 95436 (jams, jellies)

Kurt S. Adler, Inc., 1107 Broadway, New York, NY 10010, (212) 924-0900 (Christmas ornaments and decorations)

Kwan Yuen Company, 7227 Telegraph Road, Montebello, CA 90640, (213) 726-1030 (wicker baskets)

MCK Basket Imports Inc., 269 Peck Street, New Haven, CT 06513 (baskets)

Makoto Imports, P.O. Box 10325, 3001 N.W. Industrial, Portland, OR 97210 (baskets)

Maryland China Company, 54 Main Street, Reisterstown, MD 21136, (800) 638-3880 (plaques, bells, desk accessories, coffee & beer mugs)

Masterpiece Studios, 5400 W. 35th Street, Chicago, IL 60650, (312) 656-4000 (personalized greeting cards)

McCann Brothers Basket Importers, 261 River St., Bridgeport, CT 06604 (baskets)

Meistergram, 3517 W. Wendover Ave., Greensboro, NC 27407, (800) 222-2600 (custom glass etching equipment)

MGR Designs, Inc., 29 Brightside Ave., East Hampton, NY 11731, (516) 757-6434

(heart-shaped boxes and quality plastic gift containers)

Midwest Importers, Box 20, Cannon Falls, MN 55009, (800) 533-2075 (Christmas decorations)

Molecule Enterprises, Box R-2, Felton, CA 95018, (408) 335-4335 (candles, wedding accessories)

Monica's Gourmet Foods, Inc., 621 E. North Street, Kalamazoo, MI 49007, (800) 843-3645 (idividually-wrapped pecan, chocolate, and almond cookies)

Most Amazing Greeting Cards, 472 Riverside Ave., Westport, CT 06880, (203) 454-9700 (pop-up greeting cards)

Mrs. Grossman's Stickers, 77 Digital Drive, Novato, CA 94949, (415) 883-2733 (decorative stickers for gift wrapping)

New England Basket Company, P.O. Box 1335, North Falmouth, MA 02556, (508) 759-2000 or (800) 524-4484 (baskets, wrapping tissue, wide selection of colored and patterned cellophane, and form-fitted shrink-wrap bags)

Nowco International Inc., One George Avenue, Wilkes-Barre, PA 18705, (215) 277-2221 (shrink-wrap equipment, iradescent wrapping film, and paper grass)

O'Hagerty's Gourmet Coffees, P.O. Box 357, Selah, WA 98942 (509) 697-9120 (pre-measured and packaged coffee in one-cup gift bags)

Olivia Wong's, 4455 Morris Park Dr. #E, Charlotte, NC 28212, (704) 545-0382 (lace decorative pillows and embroideries)

Pacific Basin Basket Company, 8928 Ellis Ave., Los Angeles, CA 90034, (213)

558-4557 (baskets)

Palacio Company, 6250 Boyle Ave., Vernon, CA 90058, (213) 582-2550 (white wicker baskets)

Palecek, Box 225 / Station A, Richmond, CA 94808, (415) 236-7730 (baskets)

Pamela's Studio One, 33 Mountain Ave. #7-G, Revere, MA 02151, (617) 289-7055 (commemorative plaques)

Peber Nodder Company, 270 Avon, Memphis, TN 38117, (901) 383-1936 (manufactures danish cookies specially packaged for use in gift baskets)

Pegasus Originals, 129 Minnie Fallaw Road, Lexington, SC 29072. (baskets, basket decorations)

Pennsylvania Dutch Candies, P.O. Box 128, Mt. Holly Springs, PA 17065, (717) 486-3496 (candies, snack foods)

Perth Pewter, Box 99, Claymont, DE 19703, (302) 798-0291 (pewter figurines)

Pioneer Balloon Company, 555 N. Woodlawn Avenue, Wichita, KS 67208, (316) 685-2266 (latex and mylar designer gift balloons)

The Printing Machine, P.O. Box 392, North Syracuse, NY 13212, (315) 437-6712 (acetate and satin ribbons)

Quality Closeouts Unlimited, Inc., 2757 Meadow Lane, Fort Meyers, FL 33901 (813) 332-2205 (importer of discount baskets)

Renie's Collections, 33445 Western Ave., Union City, CA 94587 (baskets)

Rodrigo's Imports, 1326 Piper Dr., Milpitas, CA 95035, (408) 263-8998 (desinger baskets)

Rowena's, 758 West 22nd Street, Norfolk, VA 23517, (804) 627-8699 (gourmet jams, cooking sauces, and almond pound cakes for gift baskets)

Royal Cathay, 570 Eccles Avenue, So. San Francisco, CA 94080, (415) 952-1333 (wicker baskets, ribbons, and heat guns for packing)

Scentations Inc., P.O. Box 511, Poahontas, AR 72455, (501) 892-4933 (potpourri, scented pine cones, boiling bags)

Siam Trading Company, P.O. Box 99430, Seattle, WA 98199 (baskets)

Sniffs, 112 Park Ave., Wind Gap, PA 18091, (800) 767-2368 (aromatic sachets, scented coasters, fragrant hot pads)

Spoontiques, 208 Tosca Drive, Stoughton, MA 02072, (617) 344-9530 (pewter and crystal figurines)

Stauffer Cheese Inc., 2819 Highway F South, Bluemounds, WI 53517 (608) 437-5598 (non-refrigerated cheese and sausage gift pack components)

Superior Coffee and Foods, 990 Supreme Drive, Bensenville, IL 60106 (800) 323-6179 (gourmet coffee)

Sweet Sheets, 3630 Fairmount Ave., San Diego, CA 92105 (800) 368-9336 (fragrance-scented lace products)

Taylor's Gourmet Food Products, 2018 S. 1st Street, Milwaukee, WI 53207, (800) 776-7107 (heart-shaped cookies, foil-wrapped or tuxedo package with bow tie)

Unique Concepts, P.O. Box 9425, Wyoming, MI 49509, (616) 530-9861 (latex and mylar balloons)

United Basket Company, 58-01 Grand Ave., Maspeth, NY 11378, (718) 894-5454 (baskets, bathroom accessories, fruit baskets)

United Coffee, 1455 Third Street, San Francisco, CA 94107, (415) 421-0087. (gourmet coffees and teas)

United Design, P.O. Box 1200, Noble, OK 73068, (800) 527-4883 (porcelain animals)

United Media Licensing, 200 Park Avenue, New York, NY 10166 (212) 692-3889 (producer of a wide range of specially licensed Garfield the Cat toys and stickers)

U.S. Games Systems, 179 Ludlow St., Stamford, CT 06902, (203) 353-8400 (playing cards, game cards)

Vagabond House, 6837 Canoga Avenue #12-A, Canoga Park, CA 91303, (818) 342-1086 (antique and collectible silver accessories for executive gifts)

Weaver Werks, P.O. Box 1085, Carmel, IN 46032, (800) 523-2082 (Red Hots and jelly beans in 20oz. plastic champagne bottles)

Wellspring, 2816-E Market Street, York, PA 17402, (800) 533-3561 (greeting cards and gift books)

Willow Specialties, 288 Martin Street, Rochester, NY 14065, (716) 325-6600. (baskets)

Wine Things Unlimited, P.O. Box 1916, Sonoma, CA 95476, (707) 935-1277

(pewter wine bottle stoppers)

Windlestraw, 150 Victory Highway, Exeter, RI 02822, (401) 294-4942 (shredded materials for creating gift baskets)

Woods of Windsor, 710 Stewart Ave., Garden City, NY 11530, (516) 222-9250 (toiletries)

Supplier Index

Use the following index to locate suppliers within each specific product category. The complete address for each of these companies is listed in the Supplier chapter.

Advertising Materials
Home Income Publishing
(see page 79)

Baking Supplies
Brown Bag Cookie Art
Northwest Specialty Bakers

Balloons
C.T.I. Industries
Gift Basket Supply World
Pioneer Balloon Company
Unique Concepts

Baskets
American Wicker and Wood
Basket Supply Center
The Basket Works
Basketville, Inc.
Blind Made Products
Carolina Basket and Wood Works
Coast Wholesale
Coe & Dru Trade Company
Contessa Manufacturing
Foley-Martens Company
Gift Basket Supplies
Gift Basket Supply World
Hill's Imports, Inc.
Kwan Yuen Company
MCK Baskets Imports
Makoto Imports
McCann Brothers Baskets
New England Basket Company
Nowco International
Pacific Basin Basket Company
Palacio Company
Palecek
Quality Closeouts Unlimited
Renee's Collections
Rodrigo's Imports
Royal Cathay
Siam Trading Company
Willow Specialties
Excelsior Incense Works
Woods of Windsor

Bath Gifts
Carolina Designs

Bisquits and Cookies
American Vintage Wine Bisquits
Cella's Sweets
Christopher Brooks Distinctive Foods
Golden Walnut Cookie Company
Grandma Pfeiffer's Inc.
Peber Nodder Company
Taylor's Gourmet Food Products

Bridal Accessories
Jamie Lynn Company
Molecule Enterprises

Candles
Aromax, Inc.
Artifacts, Inc.
Biedermann & Sons
Excelsior Incense Works
Molecule Enterprises

Candy
Bitterman's Confections
Creative Concepts
Harry London Candies
The Jack Company
Koppers Chocolate Specialty Company
Monica's Gourmet Foods, Inc.
Pennsylvania Dutch Candies
WeaverWerks

Ceramics & Crystal Gifts
The Bug House
Maryland China Company
Spoontiques
United Design
Vagabond House

Chocolate
Birin Chocolates
Bitterman's Confections
Ernex Corp.
Harry London Candies
Koppers Chocolate Specialty Co.

Christmas Decorations
Creative Arts Flowers
Kurt S. Adler, Inc.
Midwest Importers

Cookbooks
American Cooking Guild

Crystal
ACC Company

Gift Books & Calendars
Chandler Press
Heartland Samplers

Glass Etching Equipment
Meistergram

Greeting Cards
David M & Company
Great Northwestern Greeting Seed
Kensington Cards
Masterpiece Studios
Most Amazing Greeting Cards
Wellspring

Herbs
Country Mixes

Incense
Aromax, Inc.

Jams & Preserves
Davidson's
Kozlowski Farms
Rowena's
Stauffer Cheese Inc.

Miscellaneous Gift Items
Comoy's of London
Flemat Company
Gifts International
Harper-Lee International
Jacquard Francaise
Olivia Wong's
Pamela's Studio One
Perth Pewter
Stauffer Cheese Inc.
Sweet Sheets
United Basket Company
United Media Licensing
U.S. Games Systems
Wine Things Unlimited

Potpourri
Aromax, Inc.
DMS Treasures
Excelsior Incense Works
Julia's Own
Scentations, Inc.
Sniffs

Ribbons & Wrapping Accessories
Brooklyn Bow & Ribbon Company
Gaylord Specialties
Gift Basket Supplies
Gift Basket Supply World
Mrs. Grossman's Stickers
NOWCO International
The Printing Machine
Royal Cathay

Shopping Bags & Containers
Gaylord Specialties
Gift Basket Supplies
Glerup-Revere
MGR Designs

Shrink Wrapping Supplies
Gift Basket Supplies
Gift Basket Supply World
Jetram Sales
New England Basket Company
NOWCO International

Silk Flowers
Creative Arts Flowers

Tea & Coffee Products
Christopher Brooks Distinctive Foods
Coffee Express Company
Fairwinds Gourmet Coffee
Great Northwestern Greeting Seed
O'Hagerty's Gourmet Coffees
Superior Coffee and Foods
United Coffee

Tissue & Shredded Paper
Four Seasons Shredding Company
Gaylord Specialties
Gift Basket Supplies
Gift Basket Supply World
Glerup-Revere
New England Basket Company
NOWCO International
Windlestraw

Basket suppliers offer a wide range of basket sizes and styles, such as those pictured here. This is one of the primary items that new gift basket makers should try to buy wholesale, since it is obviously something that most gift baskets have in common, and thus it makes sense to buy them wholesale for a reduced price per basket.

F38

F39

Custom-printed mugs and cups such as these often make a highly-appreci-
ated addition to any gift basket. If you can't find a local engraver to do these
for you, you can add to your profit margin by buying engraving tools and
etching the mugs and glasses yourself.

F69

F68

Advertising and Marketing

Fortunately, a gift basket business can get off to a great start simply through word-of-mouth advertising: You'll deliver a basket to one gift recipient one day, and that person will often call you back soon afterward to order a gift for the person that sent them the basket. It's almost as if every basket you deliver will help pick up one new customer, since the recipient will become aware of your service the minute he or she receives the gift basket.

But although much of the business will come from word-of-mouth referrals, a good advertising campaign will help the gift basket service expand and attract more new customers. Since your gift basket company is a service-oriented business, and one that you'll probably start on a small scale out of the home, advertising will become one of the most significant month-to-month expenses.

The most inexpensive approach to advertising is to use some grassroots marketing techniques that require more in the way of time, rather than money, and can begin adding to your customer list right away. Setting up an inexpensive booth at local swapmeets, for example, can be a good way to get some public exposure for your new business. This is especially effective on weekends before Valentine's Day or the Christmas holidays. Have a number of ready-made sample baskets on hand at the booth and make sure to let customers know that you offer personal delivery on local orders and can also ship baskets anywhere in the country.

Another approach that's proven effective is to place sample gift baskets in the offices of businesses which have a high number of walk-in clients, such as doctors, dentists, nursing homes, etc. Next to the basket, place a small plastic business card holder with twenty or thirty of your business cards. Offer the basket as a gift to the office, on the condition that they keep it displayed in their lobby for a certain period, such as a month or two. And make sure to have the basket securely shrink-wrapped, so that nobody can nibble at any of the goodies until the display period is complete.

As you begin to bring in more orders, don't be afraid to spend money to advertise. No business can grow to its potential unless customers know that it exists.

Most successful gift basket shops have found two primary types of advertising to be most effective: display ads in their local Yellow Page phone directory and direct mail campaigns to local homes and businesses. This doesn't mean you should rule out other methods of publicizing your gift baskets, such as newspaper and radio ads, but you should allocate a good percentage of your ad budget to Yellow Pages and direct mail.

How to Create Yellow Pages Ads
That Make the Phone Ring

The great advantage to the Yellow Pages is that anyone who has gone to the trouble to pick up the phone book and look under the "Gift Baskets" heading for a gift basket shop is obviously a very qualified and motivated buyer. Thus, you don't have to waste space in your display ad to sell this potential customer on the concept of gift baskets in general. Instead, your primary concern in a Yellow Pages ad will be to get this potential customer to call your gift basket shop before calling any of your competitors.

Usually, a business can select from three different types of ads in the Yellow Pages. The basic advertisement is the straight listing, which is provided free. For an additional fee, you can get the name of your gift basket company in bold type and a small description of your service written underneath the listing. This is usually always worth the small added cost, considering that a regular listing in plain type can easily be overlooked by the consumer.

The second type of listing is the "space ad," which spans across one column only and runs from 1/2 to 2 inches in height. This type of ad can have large type and a hairline border around them, and offer the extra room to put the phone number in larger bold face type.

The next step up from the space ad is the display ad, which can vary in size from one quarter of a column to half a page. These understandably cost more than the other types of advertising, but offer the large space needed to use custom artwork, large type, and a detailed description of the benefits of a particular company. With many directories, display ads can make use of a second color ink in their design and often receive a complimentary cross-reference in the alphabetical listings that says "see advertisement this classification."

One call to the sales reps at your local phone company will show you how Yellow Page advertisements can be very expensive, especially in large metropolitan phone books. This means you can't afford to waste ad dollars on boring, generic ads that simply state the company's name and phone number and maybe a few of the types of baskets offered. Use this ad space to aggressively sell the company and stress its benefits it offers *to the customer*, in relation to present and future competitors within the local market.

Don't waste money running trite, empty slogans like "Best Gift Baskets in Town" or "We Aim to Please." Instead, pinpoint the unique selling position of your gift basket company and demonstrate how you will provide the customer with a better deal than he or she can find with the other gift basket and flower shops that compete with you. Do you offer a wider selection of basket designs? Lower prices? Do you deliver? Do you also offer balloon and accessory gift items?...These are the things you need to let customers know, since it will definitely influence their decision to use your gift basket service.

Some other Yellow Page advertising tips: First, have a memorable phone number, if possible. Numbers in sequence (2-3-4-5) or in pairs (2-2-4-4) are easier for customers to remember. Second, don't be afraid to put a lot of copy in your display ad, since research has shown that long copy ads outpull short copy ads in the Yellow Pages.

Targeting Your Market Through Direct Mail

Mailing your advertising message to the homes around your gift basket shop can be one of the most effective methods of reaching the people most likely to buy the baskets. With a local direct mail campaign you pay just to target the houses within your geographic vicinity, unlike running an ad in a large metropolitan newspaper or magazine, which covers a broad area outside of your market.

An effective direct mail campaign requires a good deal of planning and "lead time" to carry out properly, as there are many steps involved, such as buying mailing lists, securing bulk mailing permits, designing and printing the mailer, and stuffing envelopes. Most merchants and businesses that want to reach all the homes within a specific neighborhood pay to rent "carrier route" mailing lists from mailing list brokers, who are listed in the Yellow Pages. These are lists of addressed labels for each of the homes on a particular postman's route.

In addition to the carrier route list rental fee, which can be from 5 to 10 cents a name, a company using bulk mail must also pay the Post Office an upfront fee of around $50 for an annual bulk mailing permit. This might seem like a hassle, especially for a small mailing of only a few thousand pieces, but it can save up to 45 percent on the overall cost of the mailing when compared to sending out the brochures with first class postage. Check with your local Post Office for details on carrier route pricing and requirements.

A good direct mail alternative to bulk mailings is to have your ad included in grouped coupon mailers, where a number of coupons from different merchants are sent together in the same envelope. Although this type of direct mail isn't as distintive as sending out your own custom-printed mailing piece, it definitely costs less. To have your gift basket shop's advertisement included in a grouped coupon mailer, for example, will cost around $300 to $500, depending upon the number of houses that receive it. For you to print your own brochure, however, and mail it out to this same number of house could easily cost over $2,000. Look in your Yellow Pages under "Advertising - Direct Mail" to find coupon mailing companies in your area.

How to Write Ads That Sell

Remember, your advertisements will compete with the hundreds of other commercial messages that bombard the average consumer throughout the course of the day, so you must strive to cut through this clutter and make potential gift basket customers notice you. Before you begin any advertising campaign, it's imparative that you study the following guidelines to create effective copy for your gift basket promotions:

Appeal to customer's emotions: Motivate customers to pick up the phone and order a gift basket. Appeal to these emotions by stressing how your gift baskets offer many benefits to them as gift givers. Talk about the way the baskets make a gift that's custom tailored to the recipient, and thus bound to more appreciated than a standard, store-bought item. Also stress the fact that many of the items in the gift basket will last a long time, such as jams and jellies, and make the recipient think about the gift long after he or she has received it. In other words, gift baskets make the gift giver look good.

Use photos: Gift baskets present a very attractive and interesting photographic subject, so never fail to include a professionally-shot photo of one of your gift baskets in your print, Yellow Pages, and direct mail ads. One photo of the basket is many times more effective than simply adding a lengthy written description of a basket to your ad. If you can't take these photos yourself, hire a photography student from the local high school or college to take both black-and-white and color photos of your "standard" ready-made baskets and some of your best custom baskets. Aside from using these photos in advertisements, you'll need to keep a photo album of your basket creations, so that you can show this to potential customers.

Sometimes, it can be difficult to get really top-quality photos of gift baskets, since the gift items inside the basket can become hard to recognize in a photo. If this is the case, try assembling sample baskets that use large, easily-recognizable items, such as champagne bottles and pieces of fruit. Also cut down on the number of items inside the basket, as this will usually look better in the finished photo than a bunch of small items.

Artist renderings of the baskets are an option to photography, and can produce a very classy finished picture. Contact an art student at the local college or high school and have them paint some of your sample baskets. This really isn't as expensive as it sounds, and an artist should charge no more than $50 to $100 per drawing to produce a watercolor for use color brochures, or a charcoal sketch if the drawing is to be used in a black-and-white brochure or advertisement. Remember, the drawing the artist does should be fairly large, on a sheet of 14" X 20" paper, for example, since this will make the photo look very sharp when the printer reduces it down to size for the brochure. Look at the watercolor picture on the cover of this book as an example of this type of artwork.

Create a sense of urgency: Motivate potential customers to act now and order their gift basket. Don't be afraid to explain in the ad exactly what you want customers to do, i.e. pick up the phone and call in their order. Try using directives like "act now" or "call now" in the copy of the ad, and especially at the end of the ad next to the phone number.

Never introduce a non-selling factor that could cause confusion: Don't put non-motivating copy in your ads like "gift baskets: a hassle-free way to give a gift" because that could make people think to themselves, "wait a minute, maybe it is a hassle to order a gift basket."

Sell by comparison: Consumers today are skeptics. They want to see proof of advertising claims and don't settle for vague hype like "Ours is Better" or "The Best Gift Baskets in Town." Show the benefits of gift baskets over other forms of gifts, such as flowers, and explain why your gift basket company is better than other gift basket suppliers in town. Don't attack or insult the competition, just concentrate on explaining the advantages you maintain over them. When you sell by comparison, you're truly communicating with prospects, who must decide to buy your product over other gift alternatives.

Keep your copy lean and filled with facts: Don't embellish your advertisements with flowery, adjective-ridden copy that spouts such puffery as "the very finest and most beautiful gift baskets of the highest quality..." This type of weak, puffed-up verbage doesn't motivate consumers and lessens the impact of the ad. Imagine a customer walking into your gift basket shop and asking "why should I send a gift basket to my friend instead of flowers?" You wouldn't answer with "because our gift baskets are the very finest and of the highest quality." Instead, you would spell out the benefits of gift baskets over other gifts, such as the way the basket can be customized to the recipient.

Avoid meaningless slogans: You might think it clever to add such trite wording as "gifts that put a smile on their face" or "a gift for all occasions" but these kinds of empty phrases only waste advertising dollars. Stick to specifics that help educate the potential gift basket customer, like "gifts customized exactly for that someone special." Strive to create a mental image in the minds of the customers that motivates them to buy your baskets.

With any type of advertising, you must constantly analyze what works and what doesn't. Always ask new customers how they heard about your business. Learn where these customer come from and what they want and gradually tailor advertisements, and the media in which you run these ads, to reach these customers.

Newsletters

Many gift basket services have found that printing and distributing their own small newsletter helps to maintain customer loyalty and get people coming back continually for more baskets. These newsletters go out once every few months to the people on the customer mailing list, i.e., everyone who has already ordered a gift basket, everyone who has received one of the baskets, and also anyone who's called up to inquire about your service. It might also be a good idea to build up a mailing list of the people at local companies who are in charge of buying corporate gifts for their company and mail the newsletter to them.

A newsletter only needs to be a small, four or eight page publication that presents articles and photos with a news "angle" to them, so that it doesn't come across as a pure advertising brochure for your gift basket company, and gets the reader interested in the new theme baskets you've created, some of the more noteworthy custom baskets you've designed, and any other interesting news. If you don't want to attempt to write this newsletter yourself, hire a journalism student from a nearby college to do it or call your local newspaper and see if one of the reporters would like to do it as a freelance job on the side. The cost to have someone write these brief articles should range from $75 for a student to around $200 for a professional writer.

Once the articles are written and photos of many of the baskets have been shot, you'll need to find an artist to help with typesetting the copy and laying out the finished newsletter so that it looks like a professional, high-quality product. Ask your printer if he knows of anyone who can help with this, or call the art department at your local community college to see if one of the graphic art teachers can recommend a talented student to help you prepare your newsletter for printing. The fee for this should be from $100 to $200, and you should try to find someone who can do the entire newsletter layout on a computer, instead of pasting it up by hand.

As you can see, to put together and mail a quality newsletter becomes an expensive, and time consuming, proposition, so most gift basket companies wait until they have a substantial customer base before investing in a newsletter. Aside from the production costs already mentioned, you must also figure that it will cost around $300 to have 3,000 eight-page newsletters printed up, and another $750 to mail all these newsletters. This adds up to a total investment of around $1,400, and although it seems like a lot of money, it has proven to be a viable means of advertising for many gift basket companies.

Free Publicity

Local newspaper and magazine editors always need fresh, entertaining story ideas to fill their pages and many new gift basket services have been very successful at attracting free press coverage of their business. Always be aware of opportunities to get this type of free publicity because readers often spend more time reading a story than they do simply glancing over an advertisement, so they're much more likely to remember your gift basket company. Also, an editorial feature conveys much more credibility than an ad. Readers are more likely to accept the information in an article as true, and less inclined to think that they're being "sold" through exaggerated claims.

The economic benefits of getting editorial coverage also make it extremely worthwhile. For example, to buy a full-page advertisement in your local community newspaper might cost $1,000, but an article on your gift basket store could easily cover that much space in the paper and cost your nothing. And your article has an advantage over any ad that you could buy: it's perceived as "news" because the editors of the publications obviously choose to write the story.

The process of obtaining press coverage is simple: Type up a one or two-page "press release" that explains your new gift basket business and includes all the facts, i.e. when you started the business, the type of baskets you sell, who your potential customers are, etc. This should be double-spaced and must be neatly typed. And strive to give the press release a "news" angle. In other words, find something new and exciting about the company that warrants news coverage. This could be your selection of unusual custom theme baskets or the fact that you're the only gift basket company in town. You will have much better luck attracting the interests of newspaper editors and television news directors if you can present an interesting news slant to your press release.

The first step to getting press coverage is obviously to have your business up and running. Don't contact newspaper or magazine editors until you've been in business for a few months. This way, you'll have already established a small client base and have a photo album full of custom basket creations to show reporters. You might also have testimonials from satisfied customers that can be included in the the press release. Even if you send out press releases announcing your "grand opening" you will still have the benefit of a few months worth of actual experience to relate in the story.

Make sure to include photos and brochures, if possible, with any press releases you send out, as this will increase the chances of newspaper editors noticing your press release among the hundreds that they receive each week. Photos will also increase the likelyhood of small community newspapers running a story on your business because these papers often don't have the manpower available to send someone out to take pictures for every story. If you supply the photos, they can simply use these photos in the article and call you over the telephone to do the interview.

Advertising Timeline

Considering the advertising methods we've just discussed, and the fact that most first-time gift basketeers start out with a very limited budget for promotional expenses, the following sequence of steps should be taken to promote the business. They are listed in the order of importance with respect to keeping start-up costs at a minimum.

1. Design and print business cards.

2. Create sample baskets to show potential customers. If possible leave some of these baskets, and a stack of business cards, in the lobbies of doctors' offices and other high-traffic businesses.

3. Photograph some completed baskets before they are delivered to customers and compile a photo album of the best looking baskets.

4. Place ad in Yellow Pages.

5. Write press release about the business and send out to local newspapers, along with photos of yourself and some of the baskets.

6. Call potential corporate accounts to find out who in their organization handles corporate gift buying, and explain to these people about your service. Follow-up by sending them a business card and a sales letter.

7. Design and print brochure or postcard to mail out to corporate accounts. Use as many photos and drawings as possible to show sample baskets. This promotional piece can also be left with basket recipients as they receive their gift.

8. Write and typeset newsletter to send out to past customers and potential corporate accounts.

Pre-Printed Color Brochures

A set of color brochures is available to help people get their gift basket service off the ground as quickly and effortlessly as possible. These 8-1/2 X 11-inch glossy brochures feature color photos of popular gift basket designs on both front and back, and have a blank space on each side where a person can attach their business card or stamp on their company name.

"Basically, this package gives you a professional image right from the start," explains Ron Perkins, author of *How to Find Your Treasure in a Gift Basket* and creator of the brochure package. "This way you have your own color brochures and look like a pro for a fraction of the cost of designing and printing these things on your own. It also saves you a lot of time in the start-up phase, since you can go out on your first day in business and use our brochures to get orders."

To get an idea of the cost savings of this package, consider that an individual gift basket service would have to spend a total of $1200 to $1600 for photography, typesetting, and printing for 1,000 color brochures (which works out to $1.20 to $1.60 per brochure). By printing in large quantities, however, Perkins can offer his brochure package at a price of only $39.95 for 100 brochures.

To find out more about these brochures, write to Home Income Publishing at 2796 Harbor Blvd., Suite 107, Costa Mesa, CA 92626. Or call them at (714) 252-7599 between the hours of 9 a.m. and 5 p.m. Pacific standard time. A sample color brochure will be sent upon request.

- PRESS RELEASE -

Date: Jan. 10, 1989

For more information,
contact Sally Johnson
at (213) 555-1200

New Service Specializes in Personalized Gift Baskets

People looking for something special to give to hard-to-please
friends and loved ones now have an alternative to spending
hours going from store to store in the mall: Sally's Gift
Baskets has opened up to provide custom gift baskets for both
personal presents and corporate gifts.

Operating out of her home here in Plainsville, Sally offers a
number of "theme" baskets for weddings, anniversaries,
birthdays, Valentine's, and many other occasions. Using a
variety of gourmet foods and gift items, she assembles the
ingredients into an attractive gift basket, complete with
cellophane wrapping and ribbon.

"All a customer has to do is tell me about the recepient and
what he or she likes, and I'll find the right things to put in
their gift basket," Johnson explains. "The end result is a gift
that's perfectly customized for a person, and that's usually
much more appreciated than a standard, store-bought product."

In the two months that Sally has been in business, she's
constructed baskets for a wide variety of customers, ranging
from a woman who needed something for her parents'50th wedding
anniversary to a construction company that needed 30 identical
baskets as presents for all their clients.

Prices range from $15 for small standard theme baskets to an
average of around $65 for larger custom baskets, depending upon
the cost of the items included in each basket.

"Most of my baskets will include food items, like candy and
fresh fruit preserves," says Johnson, "and many will have a
bottle of wine and custom-engraved wine glasses. People really
seem to like personalized feeling of this type of gift."

Sally's Gift Baskets operates on a phone-in basis, where orders
are phoned in and she then drives to the customer to deliver
the basket when it's done. Interested gift-givers can order a
basket by calling Sally at (213) 555-1200.

- page 1 of 1 -

Sample Press Release: *Your press releases should be typed and double-spaced.
Always try to create a "news" angle, so that the editor reading it will consider your
announcement worth publishing. Also, notice how it's written in the third person.*

SAMPLE DIRECT MAIL PIECE FOR HOME-BASED BASKET BUSINESS

Wendy's Gift Basket
200 S. Oak St.
Lewiston, PA 01043

Postage
Stamp

Joanne Smith
100 Main Street
Youngstown, PA 01002

Custom Gift Baskets: The Gift That's Always Appreciated

FRONT SIDE

Give Someone Special a Gift Made Just For Them

Custom gift baskets make the ultimate gift and are loaded with treats that will be used and appreciated for weeks. When it comes time to send a gift to someone you love, call us and we'll work with you to create the perfect gift basket. Choose from our wide selection of gourmet foods, wines, preserves, and many other quality gifts.

Custom Theme Baskets For:

Birthdays	Mother's Day
Weddings	Birthdays
Bachelor Parties	Christmas
Anniversaries	Thanksgiving
Valentine's Day	Business Gifts
Father's Day	Secretary's Day

Call Now to Order Your Basket: (215) 555-1212

Wendy's Gift Baskets

BACK SIDE

Custom Gift Baskets
The Most Appreciated Gift You Can Give

Original Theme Baskets
for These Occassions:

Weddings	Father's Day
Thanksgiving	Hannukah
Birthdays	Bachelor Parties
Christmas	Business Gifts
Valentine's Day	Anniversaries
Mother's Day	And Many More...

Baskets to Fit Any Budget!
Free Delivery Anywhere in the City

Call Now to See Sample Baskets and
Receive a Free Estimate. See Why Wendy's
Gift Baskets Offers the Most Creative and
Affordable Gift Baskets in Town.

Wendy's Gift Baskets
200 S. Oak St.
Lewiston, PA 01043

(215) 555-1212
Corporate Accounts Welcome

SAMPLE YELLOW PAGES ADVERTISEMENT FOR
HOME-BASED GIFT BASKET COMPANY

Glossary of Advertising Terms

The following glossary explains some of the most frequently-used advertising terms. As your gift basket service expands and you try new advertising media, you will undoubtedly hear these words and terms from the graphic designers, newspaper ad salespeople, and printers that help create your company's advertising.

Advertising contract: A written agreement between a supplier of advertising, such as a newspaper or radio station, and an advertiser. This agreement usually specifies all the exact details of any advertising purchased, such as cost, date of publication, size of ad, etc.

Advertorial: A paid print advertisement that is designed to look similar to an editorial article. Advertorials often have columns of type and photos that match the typestyle of the publication in which they are placed, and accordingly, most publications require that the words "paid advertising" be clearly indicated somewhere on the advertorial.

Agency Commission: This is the fee that an advertising agency charges its client for the service of buying media to place the advertising. This fee is derived as a percentage, normally 15%, of the "gross cost" of the ad. For example, if an ad agency buys a newspaper ad for a gross cost of $100, the client pays the agency the full $100, but the agency retains 15% of this amount, or $15 in this case, and pays the newspaper the "net cost" of $85.

Bleed: When the photo or other artwork of an ad covers the entire page of a publication and leaves no margin, it is referred to as a "bleed ad."

Blowup: Enlargement of a photo or piece of artwork through any photographic process.

Bold Face Type: Typset words in an advertisment that are darker and thicker than the surrounding copy and therefore attract more attention from the reader.

Bulk Mail: Catalogs, flyers, and other advertisements that are mailed in large quantities for a reduced rate. A special permit is required form the Postal Service in order to mail items at third-class rates.

Camera-Ready: Refers to advertising artwork that is completely ready for printing. In other words, all typesetting, photo screening, and layout is complete.

Carrier Route Presort: A special class of direct mail that separates outgoing advertising mailers into bundles according to the specific postman's delivery routes within a ZIP code. Because this relieves the Post Office of much sorting labor, it is the least expensive type of direct mail.

Circulation: The total number of readers of a newspaper or magazine. "Paid circulation" refers to the number of people who have paid to subscribe, versus the "controlled circulation," which indicates the number of people who are mailed the publication at no charge.

Color Separation: In advertisements using color photography, the color photos must first be separated into film negatives of the four "process" colors, cyan, magenta, yellow, and black, before they can be printed. The printer uses a special color scanning machine to make these separations.

Column Inch: The unit of measure by which newspaper advertising space is sold. A column inch measures one inch high by the width of a particular publication's column.

Copywriter: Someone who writes the words, or copy, used in an advertisement. Once the words have been finalized, a graphic designer will usually take over and design the overall layout of the ad.

Demographics: Term used when researching the readership profile of a particular publications to find out their average age, sex, income level, etc.

Editorial Mention: Written copy that is inserted free of charge in a publication that talks about a new product or service because it is relevant to the subject matter covered by the publication.

Font: The characteristic style of a certain typeface when it appears in the finished ad or editorial. For example, the type in this book is set in a font known as "Palatino."

Four-Color Process: Color printing that uses the four basic printing colors: cyan, yellow, magenta, and black, to form a color photograph.

Galley Proof: typeset copy submitted for proofreading prior to the actual printing of an advertisement for editorial piece.

Halftone: The process in which a photograph is converted, or screened, to prepare it for printing. The halftone breaks up the image into a series of dots so that the finished photo can be correctly reproduced when printed. Use a magnifying glass to examine a newspaper photo to see examples of this halftoned dot pattern.

Illustration: the visual element of an advertisement. Often used in conjuction with the headline to grab the reader's attention and make the ad more interesting.

Insertion Order: A written contract specifying the placement of an advertisement in a magazine or newspaper. The insertion order outlines the size of the ad, cost, issue of publication in which it is to be inserted and all other important details.

Island Postition: The placement of an ad on the page of a newspaper or magazine so that it is completely surrounded by editorial and therefore doesn't share the page with any other ads.

Italic: Type style that slants to the right and upward, *such as this.*

Logo: A company's unique symbol that is used on stationery, labels, and advertisements.

Makegood: Credit given to an advertiser by a newspaper or other advertising medium as compensation for a paid ad that was run in error or not according to the advertiser's instructions.

Pass-Along Circulation: The estimated added readership a publication assumes it incurs from paid subscribers who pass along their copies of the magazine or newspaper to friends to read. Many magazines figure their pass-along readership to be just as large as their paid subscriber readership.

PMS Colors: (acronym for Pantone Matching System) Standard scale of various shades of ink color created by printing specific proportions and densities of the primary ink colors. PMS colors are used by graphic designers to show their printer exactly what colors are to be printed in an advertisement.

Point Size: Refers to the measurement used to indicated the size of typeset copy. There are 72 points to an inch, so 72-point letters are approximately one inch in height. The type of this sentence is 12 points in size.

Rate Card: The brochure published by a magazine or newspaper that shows in detail all the various costs of advertising in that publication, based on the size of ad, position in the magazine, number of insertions per year, and any special discounts applicable.

Stripping: Process of assembling negatives of photos and copy to form the composite negative from which a printer's plate is made.

Tear Sheet: Page torn out of a printed newspaper or magazine and sent to advertiser as proof that an ad was run in a specific issue.

Typesetting: The process of converting handwritten or typed words into fineshed copy ready for printing in an advertisement or article. Typesetting can be done with phototypesetting machines or computers that have graphics capabilities. This type in this book, for example, was typeset in the Palatino font, at a 12-point letter size, prior to printing.

Word-of-Mouth Publicity

In the previous chapter we discussed a number of ways to spend money to advertise a new gift basket business. Most of the profitable gift basket services use these methods, and also rely on some very important person-to-person selling techniques that require only an expenditure of a little bit of time, and not money, in order to bring in new business.

Networking and telemarketing represent the two primary ways to generate word-of-mouth advertising. Each of these sales methods requires a little practice to perfect, but can produce truly outstanding results when compared with the actual amount of time spent.

Networking

To people without a backround in sales, the idea of "networking" for business leads might sound as if it requires the business owner to be pushy and launch into an extended sales pitch with every person he or she meets. But this is far from the truth. Networking simply means letting people know about your business and what it offers.

At its most simple level this could mean nothing more than telling relatives and friends about the new gift basket business and giving them business cards to hand out to their friends and relatives. It's also a good idea to inform any business contacts about the new venture, such as the family accountant, attorney, doctor, dentist, etc. Often, these people could become customers themselves, or at least they might have some ideas on other potential gift basket customers.

If you think you don't have the time to network, try to set aside a specific amount of time each week to attend some type of business-related mixer or other social event. The local Chamber of Commerce will usually be able to give you an idea of upcoming events, such as Rotary Club meetings, Toastmaster mixers, etc.

When attending these events always bring a supply of business cards and make sure to pass them out to each person you meet. Even if you don't like the idea of selling, keep in mind that you don't have to be pushy. When you tell someone about your business, you're giving them valuable information that they might need in the future. Everyone needs to give gifts at some point during the year, so they could be very appreciative of learning about your gift baskets.

Remember that when introduced, people will invariably ask "what do you do?", so use this opportunity to explain the gift basket service and hand out a card. And make sure to get the other person's business card too, since they can be contacted later for potential business before a big gift-giving occasion, such as Christmas or Secretary's Day.

And don't just stand back and wait for people to come to you when at a networking party or meeting. Make the effort to walk up and introduce yourself. Find out what other people do for a living and learn a little about them before talking about yourself and your gift basket company. When you introduce yourself, make sure it's clear exactly what you do. For example, if the name of your gift basket company is somewhat vague, like "The Golden Basket" or some other such name, don't automatically assume that people can deduce that it's a gift basket company just from the name. Make sure to mention that you make custom gift baskets for businesspeople to give to their clients.

A key to successful networking is to be consistent and steady in your effort. Don't be too eager at networking functions, and frantically try to meet every last person in the room, or you might turn some people off. And don't try to attend too many such events each month, or you could get burned out and lack enthusiasm when meeting new people.

Telemarketing

The idea of "cold" calling strangers may make some first-time business owners hesitant, but the telephone can be a vital marketing tool for the gift basket business, and therefore some type of telemarketing program should be included in the overall advertising plan.

The big advantage with using the phone to contact potential customers is that it puts you immediately in touch with your prospects and therefore is much more personal than other forms of promotion, such as flyers or newspapers ads. Likewise, a telemarketing campaign also provides more direct feedback from the public, so you can begin to see what objections, if any, people might have at first to using a custom gift basket service, and learn what questions most consumers have about your business. This information will help when creating Yellow Page and other advertisements.

Another big advantage to the telephone is that it's inexpensive and fast, since you can begin to reach potential customers over the phone the first day you open up shop, whereas you might have to wait weeks, or even months, for a print advertising campaign to begin to take effect.

A profitable telemarketing campaign will consistently produce new customers, but this requires a good deal of planning and organization prior to just picking up the phone and making the first call. The first step is to pinpoint an exact goal to be reached through telemarketing: Do you want to talk with 10 potential new corporate accounts each day? Do you want to find a certain number of new customers each week? If you set a definite goal, it will be much easier to stick with your telemarketing program on a long-term basis.

After setting a specific business goal, write out a phone script of what you would like say to each prospect. It's usually best not to make this a script that's blindly followed word for word, but rather make this an outline of the key points you would like to cover in the conversation, such as: explaining your company, asking where they buy their corporate gifts now, finding out if they would like you to send a brochure on your company, and also asking when a good time would be to call back after they've seen the brochure.

To identify prospects, look through the local Yellow Pages and circle businesses that would conceivably buy gifts for their clients, such as dentists offices, attorneys, accountants, etc. (refer to Market chapter for more ideas). Also, think about contacting any large companies in your area, since they often have employee services departments that might post one of your brochures on their bulletin board if you offer a special discount to company employees.

Two approaches can be taken to the actual call process: the caller can simply call a prospective company, ask to speak with the person in charge of corporate gift buying, explain to this person about the gift basket service, and, finally, offer to send out a flyer or brochure. Another approach is to call first simply to find out the name of the person who handles corporate gift buying at the company, then mail out the brochure to this person. A week or two later, follow up with the phone call and talk to the person who was sent the brochure. By this time they will hopefully have looked at it and therefore will be better informed about your gift basket company when you finally talk to them to find out about their coporate gift needs.

When on the phone, always try to listen to the customers and get them involved. Nothing is more of a turn off than a phone salesperson who just reels off a sales pitch in a monotone voice. So, slow the pace down when you first make contact with prospective customers and ask a question or two to make them stop and think about what you're saying. Even a simple question can help break the ice, like "have you thought about the type of gifts you might want to give to your clients for the holidays?"

Part of the acquired skill of telemarketing is learning how to find the right person to speak to within the organization. Every business has different types of people handling the selection of corporate gifts. With some small professional companies, for example, the owner might actually choose these gifts, or the owner's personal secretary. With a larger company, it could be someone in the personnel department or the public relations department.

Keep in mind that there are certain times of the day and week when people tend to be the busiest, such as mid-morning on most days and all day on Monday and Friday. Often, a good time to call busy executives is early in the morning, before they've had a chance to get too wrapped up in the day's work and during the lunch hour, since many busy people don't go out to lunch. Also, try calling right before five o'clock, since people tend to be a little more relaxed at this time.

Once your telemarketing campaign is up and running and you've found out what sales script approach works best, a final step would be to hire other people to make calls for you. These people would receive a base hourly wage, plus a commission of five to ten percent on any sale they bring in. Having other people making telemarketing calls for you will free up your time to manage the business and ultimately allow you to expand your customer base to a much greater extent than would be possible with just one person making the calls and handling all the other daily chores of a gift basket service.

When choosing a telemarketer to make calls for the company, pay close attention to this person's phone voice and personal demeaner. He or she will often be the first contact many customers have with the company, so it's imparitive to make the best impression possible. And don't be too reluctant to pay a healthy sales commission to the phone sales people you hire, since the added incentive will usually make them work harder and bring in more gift basket orders.

GIFT BASKETS

The Basket Case

Custom designed gift baskets
for all special occasions

Dee Wilson • (617) 555-6742
3400 Maple Lane, Culverton, MA 01218

Wendy's Gift Baskets

Personalized gift baskets
for any occasion:

- Christmas   • Bridal Showers
- Birthdays   • Romantic Gifts
- Anniversaries   • and much more!

Wendy Johnson

223 Main Street, Yorktown, PA 19001 • **(215) 555-4533**

Cards shown at actual size of 3-1/2 X 2 inches

Business cards can be your most effective, and inexpensive, form of self promotion. The top card shown here is made to fit in a customer's Rolodex file, while the bottom card is a standard-sized business card. As with all types of advertising that you create for your gift basket service, use a photo or drawing of a gift basket as part of your business card if possible. This makes the card more likely to get noticed and remembered by potential customers. If you can, find a graphic designer or art student to design the cards—it's worth the small extra cost to do it right.

Facility

Starting at Home

Gift basket assembly provides an ideal home-based business: Orders come in over the telephone and you go out to deliver the baskets to customers, so customers will rarely come in to order baskets in person. This is one of the primary factors that contribute to the low start-up costs of this business, since you don't need to rent a storefront shop at the very beginning. As your business grows and cashflow increases, you can expand into a retail store to attract more visibility in your community.

To set up the business at home, establish a specific area—perhaps in the garage or a separate room—that's dedicated exclusively to the basket assembly. You'll need a large, sturdy worktable on which to assemble the baskets. It's also a good idea to have plenty of shelf space at your disposal to provide storage room for empty baskets and many of the ingredients that are bought in bulk to include in the baskets. Some gourmet food products and fruit items require a refrigerator for storage, and if the space in your kitchen refrigerator proves to be in short supply, you might consider finding another refrigerator to set up in your gift basket room.

Of course, you'll need a place for your business telephone and telephone answering machine, plus a spot for your personal computer if you plan to maintain your business records and customer files on this type of machine. And if you can manage it, a separate door from this room to the outside of the house is an ideal set-up, so customers who come over won't have to walk through the house to get to your "office." Of course, if you set up in a garage you'll have the garage door as a separate entrance.

Once you start running the gift basket service from your home, you can deduct a portion of the rent or mortage as a business expense, as long as a specific room or area of the house is used exclusively for the business. This holds true whether this portion of your house or apartment is used to meet or deal with customers, or if it's an area where you actually assemble the baskets.

For example, if you pay $400 per month to rent a two-bedroom, 1,000-square-foot house, and you use one bedroom (250 sq. ft.) exclusively for your gift basket business, then you should be able to write off 25% of your rent, or $100, as a business expense, since 250 sq. ft. represents 25% of 1,000 sq. ft. Other expenses you can deduct include a percentage of the total amount paid for: real estate taxes, mortgage interest, utility costs, home insurance, and depreciation of the specific area used for the business. Refer to the Accounting/Legal section of this book for a more detailed explanation of this important tax advantage.

The Hidden Costs of Working at Home

Although starting a gift basket business from the home definitely saves money on rent and other related costs, there are some "hidden" costs to operating a business from the home, and these costs need to be considered when trying to decide whether to start the gift basket service from the home, or rent a small storefront and set up right from the start as a retail store.

First, think about the extra business you would undoubtedly receive if you operated out of a retail store. You would present a much more professional image and have the display space necessary to show a number of sample baskets and really get customers excited about your products. You would also attract many drive-by and walk-by customers who just happened to be passing the store and become interested enough to stop in and check it out.

When working out of the home, you really wouldn't want many customers coming to your home on a regular basis to look at baskets, so you will have to go out to them and show them samples from your brochures and photo albums. The bottom line is that your sales potential will be much higher from a retail store and you could be losing a large percentage of your possible market share by remaining a home-based business for too long.

Other hidden costs include the extra money you should set aside from your profits each month to save up for future expansion to a retail store, and for educational products, such as seminars and books, that you'll buy throughout the year to keep up to date on the art and business of gift basket making. Figure on adding an additional 10 percent into the gift basket prices to account for these two long-range expenses.

As a home-based businessperson, you will also generally have to put a greater percentage of revenue back into promotion and advertising than many of your storefront competitors. This is because a store maintains a high degree of visibility in the community and its very location is, in effect, a form of advertising in itself. So, starting from home will be cheaper at the beginning, but if you plan to make a long range commitment to the gift basket business, plan to move to a storefront at some point in the future.

Expanding Into a Retail Storefront

It's admittedly a big step in any business to move from a home-based office into a retail commercial space, but the ultimate expansion of a gift basket business usually requires this transition after a solid customer base has been built. By becoming a "real" shop, with a leased store on a busy street, you will attract many times the customers to the business and make it more convenient for the customers who come into your store to pick out their gift baskets. Also, new customers will often be more confident about your abilities and professionalism if they walk into a regular storefront instead of a garage or home office.

Aside from the added expense of leasing the store, moving to a retail location also introduces some other new circumstances and conditions to consider. For example, you'll now have to put some serious thought and effort into setting up an attractive showroom and arranging sample baskets for display. You must also consider how the new store location will attract the maximum amount of drive-by and walk-by traffic. These people represent the impulse buyers who you can't be reached by working out of the home.

Although some gift basket proprietors have established successful business locations in non-retail office space and relied upon advertising to bring customers into the showroom, most basket makers eventually move from a home-based to a retail location in order to build more visibility for their operation. A highly visible retail location, of course, will provide this visibility more readily than out-of-the-way office space, but will generally cost a little more on a per-square-foot basis.

Committing to a yearly lease might seem like a frightening proposition to some first-time business owners, but there are ways to reduce the financial risk and maximize the benefits of a store lease. First, investigate the possibility of subleasing a small space within an existing gift store or gourmet food shop. If these business has the room to spare and doesn't already offer similar services, you might be able to sublease a few hundred square feet on a month-to-month basis.

When approaching a store owner to propose this arrangement, keep in mind that both parties must benefit from this type of sublease in order for it to work: Your gift basket business can benefit from the foot traffic generated by the larger store and the fact that customers coming into this larger store might not have thought about gift baskets until seeing your display within the store. With a sublease you also can often rent month-to-month, which means less of a financial commitment.

The store subleasing to you obviously benefits by picking up a little bit of income from the rent payments. More important, however, is the fact that the gift basket display in their store will attract customers that have come in specifically for gift baskets, but could end up buying other items in the store on impulse. Thus, it becomes a synergistic relationship, with both the main store and the subleasee bringing in potential customers for each other's business. Also, if you locate the sublease within a gourmet food shop or some other type of establishment that sells ingredients that frequently go into gift baskets, you could guarantee the store owner that you will purchase these items from him.

Analyzing a Potential Retail Market

By the time you're ready to consider moving up to a retail storefront, you will usually have been in business for a while and gotten a good idea of exactly who your customers are and how they found out about your gift baskets. This is certainly a solid foundation of market research, but it's only the beginning: When you make the conversion from home-based gift basket service to retail shop, you're now in the same league as the other gift-oriented retail businesses in your area. Because of this, you must carefully analyze the overall retail gift market in your neighborhood to see what part of town offers the highest concentration of customers and to predict the general business climate and make sure it's a good time to launch a retail store.

Begin your formal market research by contacting the local chamber of commerce for information on the population growth and financial climate of the neighborhood in which you plan to open up a gift basket retail store. A large plant shut-down or company lay-off in the area could seriously curtail the retail activity for awhile, and contribute to a declining local population with less descretionary income for gifts. You can also get some of this information from local newspaper and radio station advertising departments, who will send out "media kits" to business owners. These media kits chart the spending habits and "demographic profile" of the people in the local community and offer a wealth of research data.

In this initial planning stage, you must make sure that the population base of your community is large enough to support a retail gift basket store and that the people within this community have the household income to afford $30 to $100 gift baskets. Whereas a home-based gift basket service can prosper in a market of 10,000 or more people, a retail operation will require a population base of over 20,000 people to generate the added business needed to support the additional expenses of running a retail store.

Selecting and Leasing the Store Site

Before signing the lease papers for the new store space you must consider a number of details about the proposed store site. First and foremost, make sure you have accurately estimated the rent-paying capacity of the business. At this point, you've already been in business for a while and thus have an idea of the monthly profit the business generates. But will you make enough extra income by moving to a retail store to cover the added cost of rent? And don't forget that moving to a rented storefront could also mean additional expenses for the part-time labor needed to mind the store while you're gone, in addition to the one-time expenses of installing all the display fixtures in the store (more on this in the Start Up section).

Next, look at the accessibility of the store to customers. Is there ample parking, and is the parking lot easy to enter and exit? Is there a median divider in the middle of the road that prevents motorists from turning left into the parking lot? Is the store located on a high-speed thoroughfare where motorists might hesitate at the thought of potentially angering drivers behind them by slowing down to enter your parking lot? If you depend on the volume of foot traffic passing by the store, note any large department stores nearby that might attract pedestrians.

Investigate the history of the particular store site you plan to rent to find out what happened to the businesses that were previously renting there. If a number of different businesses have rented that space and failed to stay in business for any length of time, there could be some inherent problems with the site location.

Try to locate your gift basket shop next to stores that will attract the same type of customer you're trying to reach, such as gift shops, flower stands, gourmet food stores, womens' clothing stores, childrens' clothing stores and other businesses frequented by women in general or men looking to buy gifts.

Even the side of the street on which the store is located can become an important factor in attracting customers. Research has found that shoppers are more inclinded to enter a store located on the shady side of the street than one where the hot sun beams in through the front windows. Also, if the store resides on a major commuter street, it will be more favorable to locate the it on the "going home" side of the street than on the "going to work" side, since commuters will have more time to stop in your shop on their way home from work.

Before committing to lease a space, sit in a car across the street and watch the other stores next to it for a day. Note the flow of customers that stop and enter nearby shops and pay attention to the type of people frequenting these businesses. Do they look like good prospects for your gift basket company? For example, if it turns out that the businesses nearby attract mostly teenagers who come in after school, you might want to consider another site.

Questions to Ask Before Signing the Lease

In addition to the points we've mentioned above, make sure to investigate all of the following check points before signing the lease:

- Can you secure the necessary zoning and building permits for any construction or alterations you intend to perform on the store building?

- Is there enough electrical power to run any equipment or refrigerators?

- Are there any restrictions on the size and design of the sign that will be put up on the front of the store?

- Who will pay utilities, such as heating, electrical, and air conditioning?

- Will the landlord allow any alterations that might be necessary to set up the gift basket shop?

- Does the health department require you to provide separate restrooms for men and women employees?

- Will you have to return the building to its original condition if your lease term expires and you choose not to renew?

- Can you ship and receive goods easily at the store site?

- Is the existing lighting sufficient or will additional skylights and electrical lights have to be added?

- Will burglary insurance cost much for this store site?

- Have you checked with the fire department to see if they'll allow you to operate your business at this location?

- Is the physical stucture of the building sound? Are there any leaks in the roof, termites, other such structural problems that must be corrected before you can begin operation of your business?

Because a lease is such a significant financial obligation, and often comes with a cavalcade of terms and conditions, you should hire an experienced real estate attorney to examine the lease agreement before you sign it.

Store Fixtures

Decorating a retail store is an art in itself. It requires a lot of thought to create product displays and an overall store layout that will attract potential customers and make them more likely to buy your gift baskets.

The first consideration is the window display. Think about who the clientele really is and what price range of gift basket they're most likely to buy. If you create a window display with large, very expensive gift baskets, you might scare away people looking to buy smaller, less costly gifts. So, start by planning a wide range of sample display baskets in many varying price categories.

If you are aiming at an upscale customer–someone who would buy a $200 or $300 gift basket–then try to go for quality instead of quantity in the window display. In other words, don't clutter your displays with a flood of small baskets and knick-knacks. Display a few expensive baskets and make sure that these baskets contain only top-of-the-line ingredients, since the people who buy more expensive gifts are more likely to know the difference between quality products and junk.

When setting up a display geared toward the upscale consumer, you must also use quality fixtures to hold your baskets. For example, displaying an exquisite, $300 basket will not have much effect if this basket sits on a cheap folding-leg table. Such classy display fixtures as oak tables, white plaster pedestal columns, and draped fabric will help accent the baskets and also lend an air of sophistication to the entire shop.

Of course, in some retail locations and markets, it may not be a good idea to zero in on just the upscale gift buyer, since there is a huge market of consumers who can't afford a $300 gift basket, but who will gladly pay $30 to $50 for a more modest basket. If this is the case, make sure to mix in some reasonably-priced baskets in the window display so that you won't scare away budget-minded shoppers.

Research has found that certain display arrangements help attract a shopper's interest and induce him or her to buy. Displays that accent vertical elevation, for example, such as pillars and ladders, have been shown to convey elegance and added value. Many flower shop owners know this and display their bouquets atop pedestals around the store.

Even on a tight start-up budget, gift basket store owners can find a number of inexpensive items to use as dispay pedestals. Old wooden crates, for example, can be painted or left in their natural condition and stacked to make display shelves for gift baskets. Cover large cardboard boxes with gift wrapping paper, or make hanging platforms that connect into the ceiling.

Also, try to think about display items that tie in with the theme of some of the gift baskets: An old-fashioned copper bathtub could make an attractive display for a few bath-related gift baskets. Or, use a Christmas tree as a backdrop to highlight sample Christmas gift baskets.

Use your display fixtures to transform the entire shape of your store space. Just a few simple fixtures can turn a boxy, drab floorplan into an exciting shop that makes customers want to stay and brouse...and ultimately buy.

Give careful attention to the "lines" of the displays, i.e., the way in which a display makes the customer's eye move and focus on the products. As we've mentioned before, vertical lines give an impression of height and value. Diagnoal, or slanted, lines, on the other hand, create excitement and usually produce a double-take from the customer.

To create a softer, richer display behind the baskets you can drape fabric over stacked display boxes and set the baskets on top of the fabric, so that the fabrick flows down from one tier of the display, under the baskets, to the next tier. When using fabric, it's a good idea to stick with rich, solid colors, such as royal blue or green, because a busy patterned fabric will detract attention from the baskets rather than accentuate them.

You also might want to use your displays to round out one or more of the corners of the store space to make it more visually interesting to the customer. As stacked-box arrangement, for example, can be made to curve from one wall to the next and thus round out the corner. Likewise, a boring, squared-off plate glass window can be made more appealing by adding drapes along the top and sides of the window.

BASIC GIFT BASKET STORE LAYOUT - 600 SQUARE FEET

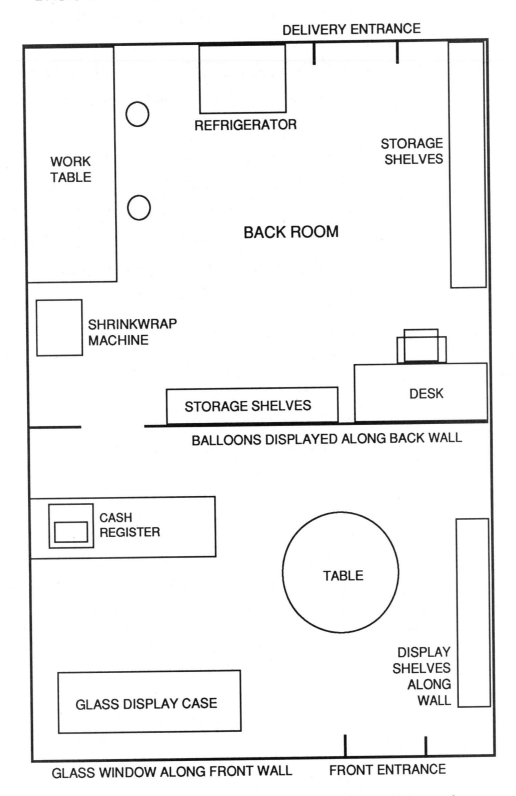

Notice that the front and rear rooms of this store are nearly equal in terms of square footage, since a good deal of room must be set aside for basket assembly and inventory storage.

Custom packaging represents another service that can be offered from a retail gift basket store. The wall of this retail store has been set up with a display showing a variety of ribbon and packaging options.

Present vs. Future Store Locations

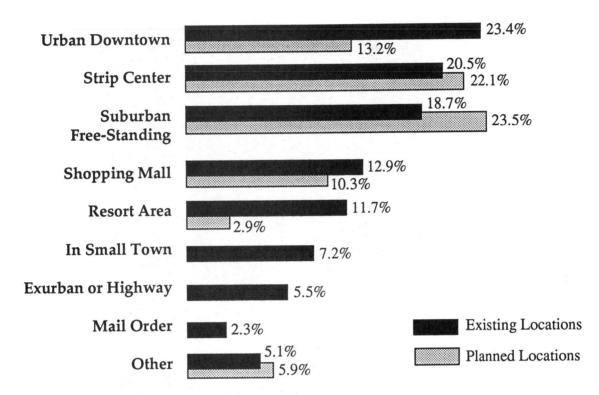

According to a recent gift industry survey, the leading locations for gift and decoratrive accessory store expansion are strip centers, shopping malls, suburban free-standing stores, and urban downtown sites. This reflects the general concensus that retailers looking to expand in the gift business seek potential store locales that offer good drive-by and walk-by traffic, local and tourist business, an upscale clientele, parking convenience, and security.

Gift basket services operating out of retail store spaces also profit from selling gift items individually, such as the various products displayed on these gift basket store shelves.

Accounting and Legal Requirements

Most people start their gift basket services as a small, home-based business, and therefore don't require elaborate accounting and legal prepartion before opening up shop. A few key considerations must be considered before starting out, however. These include: deciding upon the name of the business, filing a ficticious business name statement and opening up a business bank account, and deciding upon the legal structure of the business.

Naming Your Business

When thinking about a name for a new company, it's usually best to come up with something that describes the service. Names such as "Joan's Gift Baskets" or "Gift Basket Boutique" convey a clear picture of what the company provides. Vague, cutesy names like "Wicker Wonderland" or "Goodies to Go" might sound fun at first, but they usually must be explained to people who haven't heard of the company before. This could inadvertently make potential customers overlook the business's advertising without realizing what it offers. With the way advertising messages constantly bombard consumers today, it's counterproductive to add to the confusion.

Many times there are advantages to using one's own name as part of the name of the company, such as "Joan Smith's Gift Baskets." This connects the name with the business itself, so that as the business grows and develops a good reputation around town, people will associate the owner's name with it.

If a business owner uses a business name other than his or her own name, most states and counties will require them to file a ficticious business name statement before opening a bank account. This is usually accomplished by registering the new name with the County Clerk's office and paying a small fee. Some states also require that this new name is published in the ficticious business name section of one of the local newspaper. Some newspapers often handle the entire process—from filing the name statement with the county to publishing it in their paper—for a fee of around $35 to $50. Try to do this early on while setting up the business, because it can be aggravating to put it off, then suddenly be unable to cash checks made out to the business until the ficticious name statement is filed and a business bank account can be opened.

Planning the Legal Structure

Every business is set up as one of three types: sole proprietorship, partnership, or corporation. The way you decide to structure the company will influence how you run it for many years into the future, so it's worth investigating the advantages and disadvantages to each of these forms of business entity.

The simplest and easiest way to structure a business is the sole proprietorship. Like the name implies, the sole proprietorship means that only one person owns the business and there are no other partners or investors. You only need to file a ficticious name statement and pay the fee for a business license. The ficticious name statement is sometimes referred to as a "D.B.A.", which means "does business as."

As far as legal matters are concerned, any lawsuits levied against a sole proprietor won't distinguish the proprietor from his or her company. This means that the owner of a sole proprietorship is personally responsible for any legal matters connected with the business, so the court can go after a business owner personally to collect on any legal judgements. Mentioning this technicality isn't meant to frighten the prospective entrepreneur, only to make them aware of their responsiblity as a business owner. With this in mind, it's always prudent to avoid buying too many supplies on credit or signing any long-term contracts unless you're committed to keeping the business going strong enough to pay for these expenses.

Many people start small, part-time businesses with their friends as partnerships, both for support and to split the start-up costs. The partnership is similar to a sole proprietorship in many ways, with the one obvious exception being that two or more people own the company instead of just one. And like a sole proprietorship, the company must file a ficticious name statement and open a business bank account. Most of the time, partners will set up their bank account so that both of their names are listed on the account and both signatures are required to make withdrawals.

Anyone considering going into business with a friend as a partner should definitely draft a partnership agreement with the other person before beginning the business. Although one should consult an attorney or accountant to learn the details of a thorough partnership agreement, make sure the agreement covers: 1) the specific job duties of each partner, since often one partner will handle marketing, while another actually makes the baskets, 2) the split on operating profits and ownership, which is usually 50/50, but could differ if one partner plans to put more time into the business than the other, and 3) the procedure for buying one partner out if he or she wants to leave the partnership for any reason.

A detailed partnership agreement might seem like a unnecessary formality to two good friends starting out in their new business, but it's very foolish to enter any partnership without a written agreement. Almost invariably, once the business is up and running, one partner will feel as if he or she is doing more work than the other one and become resentful. If the partnership agreement clearly states the job duties of the respective partners, however, it can help alleviate any resentment because it makes it easier to monitor if both partners are in fact doing their jobs. Also, many banks require a copy of the partnership agreement to be on record if two or more partners have access to the bank account and can sign checks for the company.

Another crucial consideration with the partnership is that fact that one partner can be held liable for the actions of the other partners. If one partner buys a large advertisement or order of supplies, for example, without clearing it with the other partner, both partners are responsible for paying goods or services bought under the company name.

With both the sole proprietorship and partnership, income is passed directly from the business to the owner or owners when it comes time to figure income taxes. So, if the business shows a net profit of $25,000, this sole proprietor of the business must show this as a personal income of $25,000. A partnership would likewise have to split this profit among its partners and each of them would be required to report their share of the money as personal income.

The final form of business entity is the corporation. A corporation exists as a separate body apart from its stockholders, and so stockholders can find some legal protection from being held personally responsible for the actions of the business. The cost to incorporate a business varies from state to state, and can run from $400 to $1,000, depending upon if a person files the corporate papers himself or hires a lawyer to do it.

Once a business is incorporated, each state usually requires that the corporation issue stock to its owners, even if this is just one person, and keep detailed "minutes," or records, of corporate meetings. The state will also levy an annual minimum corporate tax that can run into the hundreds of dollars, even if the corporation doesn't show a profit. The corporation will also be required to pay taxes on its net income, so a problem of double taxation can arise if the corporation pays it owners, who claim this income on their personal 1040 form, then pays the corporate tax. Eventually, the corporation owner could pay personal income taxes on money that's already been taxed once as corporate income.

Although some people automatically assume that a new business should incorporate because a corporate structure will protect the personal assets of the owners from any lawsuits against the corporation, this is not necessarily the case. The principal stockholders of a closely-held corporation can, and often are, sued for the debts of their company, since their lenders and creditors often require them to personally guarantee any loans or purchases made on behalf of the corporation. So don't blindly decide upon setting up a gift basket service as a corporation just because you heard that it would completely protect your personal assets.

Some entrepreneurs try to limit their personal liability by placing their personal assets, such as a car or house, in the name of their child or spouse. And, in the case of most business loans made by banks, assets held jointly by husband and wife cannot be confiscated by a lender unless the lender had both spouses originally sign the loan. But, most lenders are aware of this and require both spouses to sign if personal assets are used as collateral for a loan.

The corporate structure does become a necessity, however, if you want to raise money for the business by selling shares to a number of investors. In this case, there are advantages to forming a "Subchapter S" corporation to limit the liability of your investors. In this case, the liability of each investor, or "limited partner," is limited only to the amount of capital he's invested. Thus, the investor doesn't have to worry about being responsible for any lawsuits against the corporation in which he's invested. It's best to consult with an accountant or attorney before deciding how to structure the business.

Keep Accurate Records

The law requires business owners to keep accurate records of all business transactions, such as expenses paid out and income earned from the business. But whether or not the law requires it, a business needs some sort of accounting system in order to keep track of profits and cash flow.

Most businesses use one of two types of accounting systems; "double-entry" or "single-entry." Many experienced businesspeople prefer the double-entry system because it goes into more detail than the single-entry system and itemizes all transactions into separate categories for income, expenses, assets, liabilities, and net worth. By entering an expense paid out, or a customer's check received, in the appropriate catagories, the business owner can continuously monitor the profitability and net worth of the company.

A single-entry system is used by many small-scale businesses and really entails nothing more than maintaining a business checkbook. The checks and deposit records serve as records for tax purposes and receipts should be kept for all cash purchases to prove that the items purchased were indeed for business use. The more organized one is when recording transactions and storing invoices, receipts, and other records, the easier it will be to figure expenses at tax time.

These records will also be referred to throughout the year when it comes time to figure the state sales tax. Most states require that business owners to get a "resale license" and pay a sales tax on all the items they sell within their state. Usually, this is done on a quarterly basis, meaning every three months. The State Board of Equalization will send out the forms, which have to be filled out and sent back with a check for the sales tax amount for that filing period. This obviously means that the business owner must keep track of how many sales were made during the quarter, and how many of these sales were made to customers within the same state (usually most, if not all, sales). Each county within a particular state may also have a small added sales tax of up to one percent that's figured in with the state tax.

Other Tax Considerations

The good news about working out of the home is that the I.R.S. allows people to write off a percentage of certain housing-related expenses if they're using part of thier home or apartment for business purposes. This becomes one of the many benefits of owning a business, because it's possible to take advantage of these tax deductions without incurring any of the additional overhead costs of renting a separate office or work area.

For example, if one uses one room or part of an apartment *exclusively* for a gift basket business, you can deduct a percentage of the expenses paid for that facility. This includes a percentage of rent or mortgage, utility bills, real estate taxes, mortgage interest, and home or renter's insurance. To calculate the percentage of these expenses that can be written off of the gross income as business expenses, take the total square footage of the house or apartment and divide it by the square footage of the area used exclusively for the business. If the apartment is 1,000 square feet, for example, and one 200-square-foot bedroom (or 20 percent of 1,000 sq. ft.) is used to conduct the business, you can deduct 20 percent of the total rent payment as a business expense. Remember, if this area is claimed as a business area, it can't also be used for non-business reasons, i.e., one can't keep a guest bed in the bedroom that's supposedly set aside for solely business use.

Keep in mind that the I.R.S. often scrutinizes deductions associated with home-based businesses, so be ready to prove any expenses in the event of an audit. Although these write-offs offer a legitimate, and definitely welcome, way to ease the tax burden, always check with an accountant or tax preparation service before claiming these deductions.

And don't wait until the end of the year to start sorting through all the business records and receipts to figure expenses that can be deducted. The business checkbook acts as a record of expenses that were paid with a check, but you should also keep a ledger book of all cash expenditures. Also, use this ledger to note any expenses paid with a personal credit card, since these can easily be overlooked when figuring taxes at the end of the year. Divide the ledger into the same categories used on the Schedule C form provided by the IRS for business income. These categories include: rent, business auto expenses, advertising, wages, freight, office supplies, business meals and travel, and fees paid for professional advice from lawyers or accountants. Organizing the expenses in this fashion throughout the year will make it much easier to calculate at year's end.

Zoning Laws for Home-Based Businesses

Before starting a home-based gift basket service, check with the state and city to see if they impose any restrictions upon people operating businesses out of their residence. Most states, for example, prohibit apparel and toy manufacturing out of the home. Many states also forbid food to be processed and packaged in the home if it's intended for commercial distribution.

Most of the restrictions placed upon home-based businesses will not affect the typical gift basket business. The majority of zoning laws that pertain to in-home services are intended to prevent the residence from becoming a health hazard or an eyesore in the community. City laws, for example, will usually prohibit home businesses from placing Yellow Page ads that list a business address that's the same as their residence. Most cities (not to mention the neighbors) also don't want home-based entrepreneurs to display any signs, or sample products, outside their house to advertise the business. And, finally, these ordinances aim to prevent a heavy flow of customers driving to, and parking in front of, a private residence that's not on a street zoned for commercial use.

As you can see, most of the zoning concerns will not affect a home-based gift basket company, since the gift basket proprietor will travel out of the home to the customer to deliver the product, and therefore won't have customers coming to the house. The one area of the law that does concern gift basket makers are the state and local liquor laws pertaining to the resale of alcoholic beverages. If any gift basket has a bottle of wine or champagne in it, these liquor laws could apply, so check with the city before including alcoholic beverages in any gift basket.

Start-Up Expenses

The following estimates are based upon two different start-up strategies: The first projection looks at the costs associated with starting the gift basket service as a home-based business, where baskets are assembled at home and then delivered to the customer. The second scenario takes into account a gift basket company that's started as a retail shop in a leased commercial space.

When examining the home-based start-up costs, remember that it is possible to launch your basket business with a very small initial investment, by starting with orders from your friends and acquaintances, if they pay in advance for their baskets. We've listed the start-up expenses here to show what to expect if you want to attract a wider share of business from the general public right from the start.

Home-Based Start Up:	Low	High
Initial Inventory: (for sample baskets)	$300	$500
Wrapping Supplies:	50	150
Business Licenses:	100	150
Advertising:	0	1,000
Business Cards	30	100
Work Bench	75	150
Phone Answering Machine:	50	100
Transporation /1st Month	30	50
TOTAL EXPENSES	**$635**	**$2,200**

Retail Gift Basket Store

Start-up Expense Estimates:	Low	High
Store Lease: (1st Mo. & Deposit)	$1,200	$3,000
Opening Inventory:	3,000	12,000
Store Fixtures / Shelves:	500	4,000
Leasehold Improvements:	500	5,000
Phone Hook-Up & First Month:	200	300
Business Licenses:	100	150
Sales Tax Deposits:	300	1,000
Advertising:	2,000	5,000
Business Cards:	30	100
Store Sign:	300	1,000
Insurance (1st 3 Months):	300	600
Part-time Salaries:	600	1,500
Misc. Expenses:	200	400
TOTAL EXPENSES:	**$9,230**	**$34,050**

The Business Plan

A Necessity for any Business

Most first-time entrepreneurs think that they only need to write a business plan if they intend to raise money to start their company. And although most start-ups do need money, it's also a good idea to compile a business plan in any case, regardless of whether or not it's being used to raise funds.

Whether planning to start a tiny home-based gift basket service or buy a franchised gift basket shop or other such "turnkey" business opportunity, a business plan will greatly increase the chances of a business' success, since it forces a person to research and take an objective look at the new business.

Almost invariably, most business plans run from 20 to 50 pages and follow a definite form that includes certain standard sections. The following outline of these sections will help to understand their importance and the order in which they should appear in the business plan:

Statement of Purpose: This is a one- or two-paragraph explanation, set by itself on the first page, of exactly why the business plan was written and submitted to the reader. For example, if the new company needs money, then state exactly how much is needed and how it will be used. Also, explain how the investment will be structured—i.e., will it be a straight loan or for an equity share of the company?

"One of the most common mistakes I see in business plans is that there is only a vague idea of how much money is needed and how it will be used," says James Keegan of Keegan Capital Development in Denver, Colorado. Keegan's company reviews business plans and helps new ventures raise money through private investors and venture capital groups. As he explains, a business plan gains a great deal of validity when it clearly states how much money is needed in the statement of purpose, and uses the other sections of the plan to detail exactly how that money will be spent and why a certain amount is needed.

For example, if you need to raise $30,000 to cover the start-up expenses of opening a retail gift basket store, the Statement of Purpose in the business plan should explain that the $30,000 will be used specifically to: cover the initial lease expenses and leasehold improvements of the store site, buy inventory, cover advertising and marketing expenses within the start-up period, and all the other itemized expenses.

Executive Summary: This one-page synopsis, which follows the statement of purpose, represents one of the most critical components of a good plan because often bankers and investors will read this part first to determine if it's worth their time to study the entire plan. This section contains a brief description of the product or service the new company intends to sell and explains why this new company will succeed in the face of existing competition.

It's also a good idea to use the executive summary to really "sell" the investor on why the proposed company offers a good investment: Can you show how it will provide a high rate of return on his invested capital? Or maybe show how this new business ties in with an existing business the investor already has in operation.

Description of Business: A detailed explanation of how the idea for your particular gift basket service was conceived and developed. Discuss any research, and industry studies that relate to the particular product and its potential for future growth. If this is already an ongoing business, talk about the history of the company's operations and how the new infusion of capital or new marketing expansion proposed in the business plan will effect the structure and direction of the company.

Marketing Plan: This represents the heart of a good business plan since you obviously can't stay in business for very long if no one buys your gift baskets. All too often first-time business plan writers skim through the marketing section with vague and entirely too optimistic ideas on who the actual customers are and how to reach these people.

"Presuming someone has covered all the basic areas of the business plan," Keegan explains, "the area that usually receives the least development is marketing—how you're going to achieve sales. New products usually only differ slightly from existing ones in the marketplace, so an intelligent and realistic marketing must be employed to attract customers to a new product."

In the marketing section show industry trends and demographic research on the type of customer who presently buys gift baskets similar to yours, and cite examples of successful product launches within your industry. For backround material, go to the business school library of a university near you and look up articles in business magazines about the type of product you plan to market and the industry in general.

And don't neglect to talk with the suppliers that you'll deal with should your business get off the ground, since they might know of companies that have tried to launch similar types of gift basket company in your market area. Suppliers can become your most valuable source of information: One man who planned to start a retail store selling nothing but sweat suits found out from a sweat suit supplier that another highly successful sweats-only retailer had drastically cut the initial marketing costs of his business by giving sweets away to the personnel of local radio stations in exchange for advertising air time.

Competition Analysis: This is another area where starry-eyed entrepreneurs often fail to do their homework. Investors look for in-depth research and realistic evaluation of existing competitors and will dismiss a business plan as amateur if it doesn't include such information.

In analizing your gift basket competition, for example, you obviously must find out exactly where the other gift basket shops are located in your proposed market area. But you also should find out which of their baskets sell the best, what time of the day they do the most business, if their business is profitable, etc.

How do you find out such specific, and confidential, information about a competing company? Obviously, if it's a retail store, you can start by simply parking across the street and watching customer traffic and the types of items most often purchased.

With non-retail business you must get more creative: talk to the wholesalers and suppliers used by your competitors and tell them that you plan to start a similar business and need to know how much starting inventory you'll need. Ask them how much product the existing companies in that business order from them each month, and where they spend their advertising dollars.

Pro Forma Profit and Loss Estimate: Most investors will skip first to this section of the plan to see what bottom line profit potential is estimated. A thorough P & L statement will take into account every possible expense that is likely to arise during the first year or two of business. Likewise, the sales projections should be very conservative and based upon research of similar operations, and not just an off-the-cuff guess.

"It's always difficult to project into the future and predict sales," reflects Joe Robinson, the author of the recently-published book *You're the Boss* and an experienced business plan writer. "Most newcomers tend to over-estimate sales projections for the first year and consequently they don't ask for enough money to tide them over during this sluggish start-up phase."

Management Qualifications: The success or failure of a new venture often depends more upon the experience and integrity of the company's management than upon the novelty of the company's product or service. Bankers and private investors will consequently take a keen interest in who handles the operations, sales, product development, and financials of the fledgling company.

In this section, an introduction of a page or two should summarize how the company's principal officers were recruited for this business and how their experience makes them especially useful to the company. Also, at the end of this section a complete resume should be included for each of the principal officers in the new company, outlining all previous work experience that relates to the new business venture discussed in the plan.

"In addition to the usual elements of the business plan, it's good to have a critical path, or timeline," adds Keegan. He explains this as a chart that shows the expected dates during the first year of operation when critical events must take place, such as raising additional money, or expanding from a home based operation into a store to handle increased inventory and orders.

All this might seem very formidable to someone who's never written a business plan, which is why some hopeful entrepreneurs sometimes pay professional business plan writers hundreds, and even thousands, of dollars to write their plan for them. Unfortunately, this is not a good idea in most cases, since the process of writing a complete business plan forces a person to do research he or she probably wouldn't have done otherwise.

And in the course of this research, people often uncover findings about their proposed business idea that force them to either change the idea drastically or scrap it all together, which is much better than finding out after investing money in the project.

	Month 1	Month 2	Month 3	Month 4	Month 5
INCOME:					
Basket Sales	$600	$1000	$1200	$1800	$2200
EXPENSES:					
Product inventory	250	350	500	750	800
Yellow Pages ad	200	0	0	0	0
Advertising	300	500	0	0	0
Phone hook-up	70	0	0	0	0
Monthly phone bill	40	60	60	70	70
Printing bus. cards	50	0	0	0	0
Sample baskets	200	200	200	100	100
Delivery expenses	75	100	100	100	100
Part-time help	0	0	0	200	200
Shrink-wrapper	120	0	0	0	0
Total Expenses	1305	1210	860	1120	1270
PROFIT or (LOSS)	($705)	(210)	340	580	930

	Month 6	Month 7	Month 8	Month 9	Month 10
INCOME:					
Basket Sales	$2800	$3000	$3200	$3600	$4000
EXPENSES:					
Product inventory	900	1400	1400	1500	1800
Yellow Pages ad	300	0	0	0	0
Advertising	0	0	0	0	0
Phone hook-up	0	0	0	0	0
Monthly phone bill	90	100	100	100	120
Printing bus. cards	50	0	0	0	0
Sample baskets	100	100	0	0	0
Delivery expenses	120	120	120	150	150
Part-time help	200	200	200	300	300
Total Expenses	1760	1920	1820	2050	2370
PROFIT or (LOSS)	1040	$1080	1380	1550	1630

Sample Pro Forma Statement: This type of "pro forma" profit and loss projection should be included in the business plan, for either a home-based or retail gift basket service. It becomes a valuable planning tool because it helps estimate how much start-up capital the business will need, plus it allows the gift basket owner to plan ahead for expenses that arise at periodic times in the year, such as the deadlines for Yellow Page advertising.

Finding the Money

Although one of the beauties of the gift basket business is that it can be started on a tiny budget, there usually comes a time when the gift basket maker wishes to try out a new advertising campaign or even expand into a storefront, which requires an additional infusion of capital. Since most entrepreneurs learn very quickly that banks are not interested in lending to small, service-oriented businesses that don't have any tangible assets to use as collatoral, a number of other options should be considered as possible sources of extra funds:

Partnerships

Two or more people often band together as partners in order to cut each of their investments, in terms of both time and money. Most of the time, the intitial partners in a gift basket business are friends who thought it would be a fun business venture to attempt, and who both plan to put in an equal amount of time in the day-to-day operation of the business.

Another approach to the partnership arrangement is to find a partner who will only put up money, but not participate in the daily business activities of the gift basket service. This is often referred to as a "silent" partner, and this type of investor, in addition to wanting to own a percentage of the business, will usually also require that the company is set up as a limited partnership Subchapter S corporation in order their personal liability when becoming a partner (see Legal chapter).

A number of problems can, and usually do, arise in the course of a partnership, however. First, many people fail to draft up a detailed partnership agreement that outlines the exact job duties of each partner and many other details. Second, one partner almost always ends up feeling as if he or she is doing more actual work than the other partner, which can lead to tension.

So, consult with an attorney before entering into a partnership to make sure the partnership agreement covers as many forseeable problem areas as possible.

Friends and Family

If you don't want to give up any equity in the business by bringing a partner aboard, then the most realistic source of seed money, next to your own personal savings, comes in the form of a business loan from friends and family members.

It's important to treat a loan from family members with the same respect as any other loan, i.e. offer a solid business plan when asking for the money and commit to a definite repayment schedule. This can help prevent the loan from causing personal tension in your relationship with the friend or relative who put up the money, and make it easier to raise additional money if the business grows and the original loan is paid back on time.

When borrowing money from a friend or member of the family, always use a written loan agreement that outlines the amount of money to be borrowed, how it will be paid back, and what happens if the loan can't be paid back (i.e., does the lendor get an equity share in the business if the loan can't be paid back on time?)

Short-Term Credit

Of course, personal credit cards can provide a source of start-up capital, although their high interest rates make this an expensive option. Nevertheless, many small business ventures are funded by cash advances from personal credit cards, especially if the amount of funds needed is under $5,000.

Another form of short-term credit is to arrange for a longer payback schedule with any vendors, such as basket suppliers, so that more cash is freed up to apply to expanding the businee. Obviously, most suppliers won't extend credit to brand new businesses and require C.O.D. payments on the first few orders, but once a relationship is established with a supplier, the credit terms might be extended longer than the usual 30 days.

If you sell a large basket order to corporate accounts and extend credit to these customers for the final portion of the payment after the baskets have been delivered, then you might be able to line up a bank loan against these "receivables". This is also known as "factoring" or "pledging" and usually only possible if you have a good relationship with the bank and have been in business for a while.

SBA-Guaranteed Loans

With a loan guaranteed by the Small Business Administration, the money is lent from a private bank and its repayment guaranteed by the Federal government. To qualify for this type of loan, a business owner must have tried to arrange funding from other sources before applying for the SBA loan, and the business must be independently owned and not a dominant business in its field.

Thousands of SBA-guaranteed loans are given out each year, with the average loan size being over $100,000. These loans offer competitive interest rates and the loan recipient can also receive free management and accounting advice. And often the loan isn't as closely tied to the collateral of the business owner as a conventional loan. The SBA-guaranteed loan also requires a lot of additional red tape, since two sets of applications must be completed, one for the SBA and one for the lending bank.

Realistically, only a gift basket service that plans to open shop in a retail storefront should consider applying for an SBA-guaranteed loan. And it would certainly help if the owner of this business has a successful track record of running a profitable home-based basket business, or working for another retail gift basket shop. The bottom line is that to qualify for this type of loan, the entrepreneur must make the bank and the SBA feel very confident in the business plan and how the money will be used, the track record of the business, and the character of the person running the business.

Small Business Investment Corporations (SBICs)

Small Business Investment Corporations are privately-held investment companies that loan money to small businesses and provide management assistance. In many respects, they share a number of similarities with venture capital companies, because they sometimes will buy stock in an emerging company, in addition to providing long-term loans. Although SBICs set the maturity dates of the the loans they make, the interest rate they can charge is set by the U.S. Department of Treasury. To learn more about Small Business Investment Corporations in your area, contact your banker, but keep in mind that SBICs, like most business lenders, usually only consider loaning money to businesses that can show an established cashflow history.

Small Business Development Corporations (SBDCs) are similar to SBIC's, but concentrate on providing loans to businesses in economically deprived areas. These loans are backed by the SBA, which guarantees their repayment. Contact the local SBA office, or state Department of Commerce, for more information.

When talking to a bank or any type of institutional lender, make sure to ask the following questions:

1) What type of loans do they offer? Do they only loan for purchases of equipment, or whill they also make cash-flow loans? Will they loan against accounts receivable? Do they make SBA-guaranteed loans?

2) What are the loan limits? Will they make loans for small amounts, or are they only intersted in lending large amounts of money to established companies?

3) How long will it take to be approved for the loan? The lender could take anywhere from a few days to over two weeks to make up its mind about your loan request, so make sure you ask about this beforehand.

4) How do they process the loan? What specific requirements does the lender typically look for when lending out money, i.e., how much equity the business owner will need in order to guarantee the loan.

5) What interest rate will they charge? Are these rates negotiable, and is it a fixed, or variable, interest rate? Will there be any up-front costs for title searches or processing fees?

Glossary of Business Terms

Agent: A person who has been granted the right to act on behalf of another company or individual. For example, a company can retain the services of a business broker to act as sales agent when trying to sell the business.

Break Even: The point in time when a new business venture earns a net profit equal to the amount of capital invested. Also refers to the time of "break even cashflow," when a business's monthly net income covers all of its expenses, and therefore the business doesn't need any additional outside investment to continue operations.

Business Opportunity: A broad-based term that includes franchises, dealer-ships, and distributorships. A business opportunity is usually sold as a system for operating a business, and can include some or all of the following ingredients: instruction manual, exclusive business territory, pre-printed brochures and other sales literature, special equipment, a initial inventory of product, and more. It can also include: affiliation with national advertising, access to national accounts, and on-going management support from the home office. The general idea behind buying a business opportunity, as opposed to starting a business independently from scratch, is that it will save time and hassles for the entrepreneur and reduce the period of time before the business operates profitably.

Business Plan: A step-by-step analysis that examines every aspect of starting a particular new business. This plan looks at such important topics as: potential customer base, start-up investment needed, personnel required, potential income, new product development, and many other crucial subjects. Most plans range from 10 to 30 pages in length.

Cashflow: Refers to the actual money a business receives from customers on a weekly or monthly basis, and the money paid out for expenses during these periods. This contrast with accounts receivable, which is the money owed to a company, and accounts payable, which is the money a business owes for expenses. Cashflow must be considered carefully when planning a new business, since it might take from 30 to 90 days to collect payment on some accounts where credit is extended. "Cashflow" also refers to the ongoing monthly net profit a business generates.

Cold Call: A telephone call or personal visit to a potential customer where no previous contact or introduction has been made.

Dealer Agreement: In many dealerships or distributorship business opportunities, a new dealer will be required to sign an agreement that outlines the terms and conditions of how he will operate as an affiliate of the company that sold him the business opportunity. These agreements often cover product pricing, territory bounderies, and use of a company's name.

Distributor: An individual or company that buys goods from a manufacturer and resells them to retail stores. Also known as a "middleman" or "wholesaler."

Financing: The origin of start-up investment funds for a new business venture. This amount can come from the entrepreneur's own savings or personal loan he takes out, or from private investors. Some business opportunity companies will help arrange loan financing for people who buy their opportunity.

Franchise: More involved than other forms of business opportunities, such as dealerships and distributorships, a franchise usually outlines strict guidelines as to how the individual franchisees can use the company name, which products they can sell, the appearance of the store, etc. Most franchises offer a proven and tested business format for the franchisee to follow and strive to reduce the inherent risks of launching a new business from scratch.

Franchise Agreement: The written agreement between a franchisor and its franchisees.

Franchise Fee: The inital premium fee paid to buy a franchise. This fee is separate from other expenses, such as those incurred for site construction, equipment, advertising, personnel, and others.

Franchisee: An affiliate who's purchased a franchised business opportunity from a parent company. The franchisee typically agrees to abide by the guidelines outlined by the parent company as to the operation of the business, advertising, products and services offered to customers, and even the interior design of the store.

Franchisor: A company that sells franchised business opportunities of its particular business. Most franchisors sell specific territories in which a franchisee has exclusive rights to open his store.

Gross Earnings: Refers to the total amount of money taken in by a business during a period of time. Also known as gross revenue.

Gross Profit: The difference between the payment received from the customer, and the immediate cost of the goods or services provided. For example a product that costs $1.00 wholesale, and sells for a retail price of $2.00, provides a gross profit of $1.00.

Net Profit: The actual profit realized by a business after figuring the cost of goods or services sold and all expenses required to maintain ongoing operations, such as advertising, rent, telephone bills, payroll, etc.

Operations Manual: A step-by-step manual given to a franchisee or business opportunity buyer that outlines how to perform sales calls, employee hiring, advertising, and other knowledge specific to a particular business.

Operator: A person who runs a business or buys a busines opportunity, i.e. the person who actually operates the business, as opposed to the company that sells the business opportunity.

Overhead: Regular and consistent expenses that must be paid by a business on a monthly basis, such as rent, equipment leases, payroll, utilities, and advertising.

Profit and Loss Statement: A month-by-month projection of the predicted net profits, or net loss, a business will incur during initial two year start-up period.

Proprietary Products: In franchising or business opportunities, this refers to products or information of which the franchisor has legal ownership. This could be anything from a brand name, such as McDonald's "Big Mac," to a patented chemical cleaner.

Protected Territory: An exclusive geographical market area assigned to an entrepreneur who buys a businesss opportunity, within which only he has the right to market his company's product.

Retail: Sale of goods in small quantities to the final consumer. Differs from wholesale, which is the sale of goods in large quantities to retailers.

Return on Investment (R.O.I): The amount, expressed as a percentage, that a business returns to its owner in relation to the total capital invested. For example, If an entrepreneur invests $10,000 to start a business and earns an annual net profit of $20,000, then he has achieved an annual R.O.I. of 200 percent.

Royalty Fee: A monthly or annual fee paid by a franchisee to the franchisor. The roayalty fee is usually figured as a percentage, typically anywhere from 2 to 10 percent of a franchise's gross sales per month.

Start-Up Costs: Total amount of money needed to set up a business and keep it running until it generates a positive cashflow.

Territory: A geographical area within which a person operates his business. Many business opportunity buyers receive the rights to their own territory, which is usually based on ZIP codes or street boundaries. Sometimes territories are designated by the population base in a given area.

Turnkey: Refers to a complete business opportunity, where everything needed to start is provided for the initial investment. Turnkey franchises, for example, often give the franchisee assistance in building the store site, training employees, advertising, accounting, and all other operational aspects of a particular business.

Uniform Franchise Offering Circular (U.F.O.C.): A disclosure document that must be filed by companies offering a franchise opportunity. It reveals the backround of the principal owners of the franchise, past legal actions, and other information important to potential franchise buyers.

Wholesale: Goods that are sold in large quantites to retail businesses, who in turn sell the goods individually to the final consumer. Many gift basket businesses order their products in bulk from distributors so they can receive a discounted wholesale price.

Start-Up Timeline:

The following list outlines the sequence of steps to take when setting up a gift basket business. Although you may not want to follow the exact order of events listed here, it should give you a basic idea of what to do when starting the business and the general order in which you should do these things. You can accomplish all of these things in a matter of weeks or months, depending upon the time each day you can devote to the new venture. However fast you dive into your new business, remember not to overlook critical planning and research in your zeal to get going.

1) **Investigate potential competitors.** Visit gift shops, grocery stores, gourmet food stores, and look through the Yellow Pages for other gift basket companies.

2) **Begin drafting the business plan** and explain the business idea to as many friends and relatives as possible to get their feedback. Many of the people you talk to at this stage of your research will become your first customers or know of other people who would be prime candidates for your service, so start spreading the word-of-mouth advertising as soon as possible.

3) **Finalize the name for your new business** and file a fictitious business name statement with the county. You'll need this in order to open up a business bank account if your new business name will be anything other than your own name. These statements are required by law to be published, so check with the local newspaper, since they often offer a service where they'll process your fictitious name statement and publish it in their paper for one fee.

4) **Line up your suppliers** if you plan to buy any of the gift basket items wholesale, since it could take a few weeks to buy items and have them shipped to you. The primary concern at this point will be to line up local supply sources for baskets, since this will be your most frequently purchased item. Also, check out local retail grocery supermarkets to familiarize yourself with the retail cost and availabl-

ity of the most common gourmet food items you'll use in the baskets. Refer to the Suppliers chapter for more information on this.

5) **Create some sample gift baskets.** Design and construct a number of "staple" baskets, or generic designs for such frequently-occuring events as birthdays, bachelor parties, Thanksgiving, Valentine's, etc. Once you've experimented with various basket arrangements and wrappings until you come up with attractive designs and special names for each of the baskets, photograph all of these baskets and create a photo album. This album will go with you when you go out to talk to prospective customers, and acts as proof that you know how to create a wide variety of custom baskets.

6) **Install a separate telephone line** in your home to handle incoming calls from customers. This allows you to answer all calls coming into this line with the company name instead of just "hello."

7) **Finish writing the business plan** and call the advertising department of your local Yellow Pages to find out their deadlines and how much it will cost you to place an ad in the next Yellow Pages. When you talk to the advertising representative at the Yellow Pages, ask him or her for their recommendations and find out if they know of any other gift basket companies that are planning to start in your market area.

8) **Open up a separate checking account for the business.** Once you start depositing checks from customers and writing your own checks to buy supplies, you definitely need a separate business checking account. This will make it much easier to separate business expenses from any personal expenses, and make it easier to figure out all business expenditures when computing income tax. Larger-format business checks, with the company's name printed on them, also look much more professional than small personal checks and therefore will help you maintain a good image with dealing when suppliers and other vendors.

9) **Set up a work area in your home** to assemble baskets and store supplies. If space permits, you might want to set up a few shelves on which to display sample baskets to customers.

10) **Begin your sales effort** by contacting the friends and relatives you consulted when just beginning to plan your business. Make sure they know that you now are in business and ready to handle their custom gift basket needs.

11) **Talk to your bank** about getting a merchant number so you can accept VISA and MasterCard credit cards. Although realistically you probably won't have the business references and financial strength to qualify to accept credit cards right from the start, you should still learn about the application process and talk to your bank about it as soon as possible, so that you'll know what the banks requires and can begin to work to meet those requirements.

It's also a good idea to get to know your banker personally when you first start your business, even if you don't need a business loan. In this way, if you ever need a loan in the future, your banker will already know about you and your business.

12) **Print up business cards** and talk to your local gift shops about setting up your cards and a sample basket in their store on the condition that you'll pay them a 10 percent referral fee for every job you get that was referred by them. If you're working on a limited budget, wait until you've sold a few baskets to friends and acquaintances before you pay to have business cards printed.

13) **Design and print a direct mail piece** to send to local businesses to promote the baskets as corporate gifts. Call each of the businesses first to find out who handles corporate gift buying and address the mailer to this person. After you've mailed the brochure to this person, call a few days later to make sure they received it and to answer any questions they might have about your new gift basket service.

In order to keep initial costs down at this point, design your direct mail piece on a computer, such as the Apple and use a high quality photocopier to copy 50 or 100 brochures at a time. Check the Yellow Pages under "Typesetting" or "Printing" to find print shops that can design these brochures for you or rent you time on a MacIntosh on a per-hour basis.

14) **Prepare press releases and photos** to send to local newspapers and television stations. Before sending out a "press kit" to a particular publication or broadcast station, call first to find out to whom you should send it. With newspapers, press releases will usually go to the editor, whereas with television stations it should be directed to show producers or news directors. Call and find out these people names so you can address your package to them specifically. A week or so after you have sent the press release and photos, follow up with a phone call to see if these people have any particular questions about your gift basket business.

15) **Look for local gourmet food shops** or gift shops that might allow you to set up a sample basket and some of your business cards in their store. Ideally, the shop you choose should have high enough foot traffic and cater to a clientele that would be in the market for gifts. The waiting rooms of doctor and dentist offices, for example, are some other good prospects for this. As an incentive to the store or business owner to let you set up your sample basket, you can give them the basket as a gift for allowing you to display it for one or two months before they take it apart and use the ingredients inside it. Or, you can offer to give them a percentage–typically around 20 percent–as a commission for any basket orders you receive as a result of the basket display in their store. If you make baskets to display as samples, it might be a good idea to put non-edible gifts in them, such as bath soap, potpourri, etc., since this will make it less likely that the baskets will be tampered with while they're on dispay. A basket of candy and nuts might prove to be too tempting, and consequently, your sample basket might not be on display too long before it's contents are consumed.

Appendix

Associations and Industry Groups:

Gift Association of America
808 17th Street N.W., #200
Washington DC 20006
(202) 223-9758

Founded in 1952, the Gift Association of America is the largest trade association catering to retail gift stores and wholesalers. They publish a newsletter and retail training manuals, and sponsor seminars throughout the year to help gift merchants improve their services, and increase the profitability of their businesses. Some of the specific benefits they provide include discount VISA/Mastercard programs for merchants who would like to accept these credit cards from their customers, low cost business insurance, worker's compensation insurance, and car rental discounts.

Gift and Decorative Accessory Association
51 Madison Avenue
New York, NY 10010
(212) 689-4411

The Gift Basket Connection
3 Juniper Court
Schenectady, NY 12309
(800) 437-3237

The Gift Basket Connection is a national delivery network for gift basket retailers who wish to increase their profit potential and accept orders for delivery in other states. These orders will be made and personally delivered by gift basket retailers in the city where the order is to be delivered. The retailer who orignally received the order will retain 20 percent of the price charged the customer, and the retailer who actually prepares and delivers the basket will keep the remaining 80 percent for her efforts.

Gift Basket Retailers International
1205 W. Forsyth Street, Suite 101
Jacksonville, FL 32204
(904) 634-0440

Gift Basket Retailers International is a trade group that helps gift basket services, including home-based companies, to do the following things: qualify to process credit cards at a low transaction fee; save money on group health insurance; participate in gift basket delivery network; receive monthly supplier resource guides; and enjoy other group discounts.

Publications:

Balloons Today
Festivities Publications
1205 West Forsyth St.
Jacksonville, FL 32204

Beautiful Banquet Decorating
Festivities Publications
1205 West Forsyth St.
Jacksonville, FL 32204

Cottage Connection
P.O. Box 14850
Chicago, IL 60614
(312) 472-8116

A newsletter published by the National Association for the Cottage Industry, this publication provides information for home-based business owners. Topics include funding sources, low-budget promotion, and various support resources.

Easy 'N Elegant Balloon Weddings
Festivities Publications
1205 West Forsyth St.
Jacksonville, FL 32204

This book helps balloon decorators polish their professional presentation skills and profit from handling many additional areas of wedding planning.

Gift Reporter

George Little Management, Inc.

2 Park Avenue, Suite 1100

New York, NY 10016

(212)532-0651

This colorful glossy magazine is mailed out free of charge each month to qualified gift merchants around the country. It's purpose is to keep gift retailers abreast on all the new trends within the industry and highlight new products from gift manufacturers.

Gift and Decorative Accessory Buyers Directory

51 Madison Avenue

New York, NY 10010

(212) 689-4411

Put out once a year by the Gift and Decorative Accessory Association, this 300-page directory lists gift suppliers and manufacturers. This book is not sold separately, but is included free of charge when paying $30 for a one-year subscribtion to the Gift and Decorative Accessory Association's monthly magazine. It includes a guide to international gift markets, trade show dates and locations, listings of permanent buying centers, and many other important facts for the gift shop operator.

Pegasus Originals

129 Minnie Fallaw Rd.

Lexington, SC 29072

A manufacturer of baskets and other gift supplies, Pegasus markets a wide range of books with plans for specific gift baskets and craft projects.

Franchises and Business Opportunities

Balloon Bouquets

500 23rd Street, N.W.

Washington, DC 20037

(800) 424-2323

Balloon Express

738 Adelaide St. W.

Toronto, ONT. CANADA M6J-1B1

(416) 362-4911

Balloon Wrap

3940-F Prospect Ave.

Yorba Linda, CA 92686

(714) 993-2295

Balloon Wrap markets a patented vacuum inflation machine that allows gift items to be inserted into inflated balloons. They market this machine as a complete business opportunity, with operations manual and sales support materials.

Dial-A-Gift

2265 E. 4800 South

Salt Lake City, UT 84117

(801) 278-0413

A national network of over 5,000 gift basket shops and other gift-related retailers who work together to provide delivery service of gift baskets to customers across the country. Dial-a-Gift's central office advertises to promote their delivery network, then receives customer calls via a national toll-free 800 phone number.

Just Baskets

1111 Kane Concourse, #511

Bay Harbor Island, FL 33154

(305) 868-8407

About the Author

Since graduating with a B.A. degree in English Literature from UCLA in 1984, Ron Perkins has published more than 200 articles on small business trends and business opportunities. He worked as a staff writer for *Entrepreneur Magazine* and acted as Associate Publisher of the first annual *Entrepreneur Magazine Franchise Yearbook*.

As an entrepreneur himself, Perkins has started a number of successful businesses, including a video rental company and a television direct marketing service.

Perkins spent over three years researching and updating information on the gift basket industry to include in this book. He interviewed successful gift basket service owners, industry suppliers, and trade groups to form an in-depth, "insider's" look at one of today's hottest service businesses.

NOTES

NOTES

NOTES